Mariam and Louisa
OF MODESTY COUTURE

21 DAYS
TO LEARN TO USE YOUR
serger

× *daily practice* ×

× *step-by-step instructions* ×

× *bonus project to get you started* ×

an imprint of C&T Publishing

21 Days to Learn to Use Your Serger

First published in the United States in 2025 by Stash Books, an imprint of C&T Publishing, Inc., P.O. Box 1456, Lafayette, CA 94549

21 jours pour apprendre à coudre à la surjeteuse © 2024 by Éditions Marie Claire - Société d'Information et de Créations (SIC)

This edition of "*21 jours pour apprendre à coudre à la surjeteuse*" first published in France by Éditions Marie Claire in 2024 is published by arrangement with SIC – Société d'Information et de Créations.

PUBLISHER: Amy Barrett-Daffin

CREATIVE DIRECTOR: Gailen Runge

SENIOR EDITOR: Roxane Cerda

ENGLISH LANGUAGE COVER DESIGNER AND LAYOUT ARTIST: April Mostek

ENGLISH TRANSLATION: Kristy Darling Finder

PRODUCTION COORDINATORS: Casey Dukes and Zinnia Heinzmann

EDITING AND REVISION: Isabelle Misery

PRODUCTION AND PHOTOGRAPHY: Modesty Couture

COVER PHOTOGRAPHY: iStock

GRAPHIC DESIGN AND LAYOUT: Émilie Laudrin

COVER: Claire Morel Fatio

All rights reserved. No part of this work covered by the copyright hereon may be used in any form or reproduced by any means—graphic, electronic, or mechanical, including photocopying, recording, taping, or information storage and retrieval systems—without written permission from the publisher. These designs may be used to make items for personal use only and may not be used for the purpose of personal profit. Items created to benefit nonprofit groups, or that will be publicly displayed, must be conspicuously labeled with the following credit: "Designs copyright © 2024 by Éditions Marie Claire - Société d'Information et de Créations (SIC) from the book *21 Days to Learn to Use Your Serger* from C&T Publishing, Inc." Permission for all other purposes must be requested in writing from C&T Publishing, Inc.

Attention Teachers: C&T Publishing, Inc., encourages the use of our books as texts for teaching. You can find lesson plans for many of our titles at ctpub.com or contact us at ctinfo@ctpub.com.

We take great care to ensure that the information included in our products is accurate and presented in good faith, but no warranty is provided, nor are results guaranteed. Having no control over the choices of materials or procedures used, neither the author nor C&T Publishing, Inc., shall have any liability to any person or entity with respect to any loss or damage caused directly or indirectly by the information contained in this book. For your convenience, we post an up-to-date listing of corrections on our website (ctpub.com). If a correction is not already noted, please contact our customer service department at ctinfo@ctpub.com or P.O. Box 1456, Lafayette, CA 94549.

Trademark (™) and registered trademark (®) names are used throughout this book. Rather than use the symbols with every occurrence of a trademark or registered trademark name, we are using the names only in the editorial fashion and to the benefit of the owner, with no intention of infringement.

ISBN: 978-1-64403-625-9

Printed in China

10 9 8 7 6 5 4 3 2 1

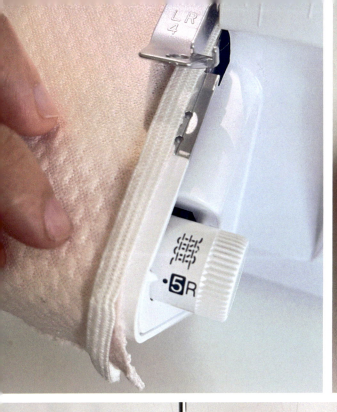

ABOUT US

We are **Mariam and Louisa**, two friends united by sewing since 2012. Not a day goes by when we don't talk about sewing or sit down at our sewing machines. This addiction (a healthy addiction, I swear!) drove us to share our passion and help others achieve their sewing ambitions because—and this may shock you—we had a rocky start ourselves.

Sure, you can learn how to sew very fast and very well if you come across the right people, but that wasn't what happened in our case. In 2012, we joined a sewing class at a local community center. Unfortunately, we were quickly lost among the other students. Everyone came with their own individual projects and we were somewhat left to our own devices. We lost a lot of time waiting for the teacher's help, and also taking on projects much too ambitious for beginners...

That's how Louisa wound up attempting a chiffon dress. I'm sure you can imagine how difficult that project was! Both the pattern and the fabric itself presented challenges. Suffice it to say, she was a heartbeat away from giving it all up and putting away the sewing machine forever.

Nobody explained to us in what order we should do things or how to build on our progress with projects that were increasingly complex but always level-appropriate.

So we turned next to free online tutorials. But this posed pretty much the same problem...It was difficult to determine which ones were at our level or not, we wasted money on unnecessary materials, and, to be frank...not all tutorials are actually any good. In short, we also learned some bad techniques. So frustrating!

Despite all this, our passion for sewing lived on! And after many years of practice, we made it our profession, and now we want to help others learn to sew quickly and efficiently. With a solid foundation, you can make nice things in no time. We've designed our courses to be progressive. Therefore, throughout their journeys, our students accomplish increasingly complex projects, which helps build self-confidence

What we're offering today with our teaching is quite simply the sort of support we would have dreamed of as beginners: we would have saved so much time and so much money!

Today, we're living our passion and it's truly a pleasure to help you learn to love sewing as much as we do.

To learn more about our courses use the QR code below or visit our website: modestycouture.com

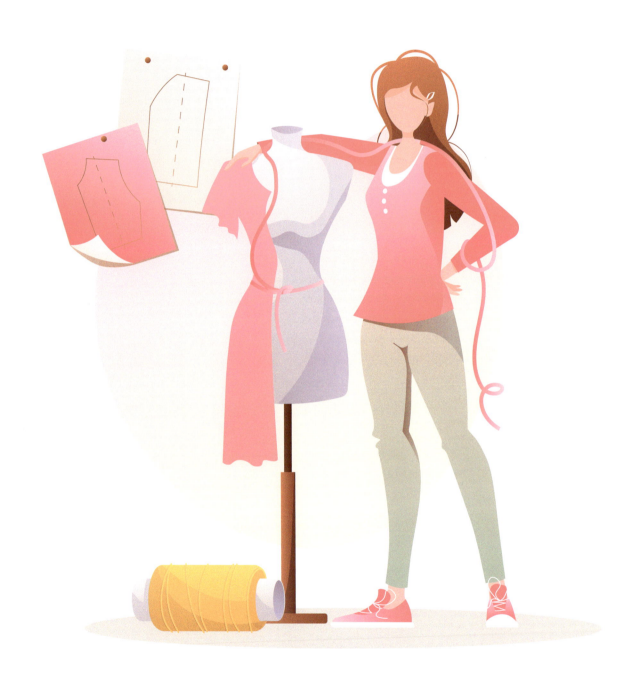

TABLE OF CONTENTS

day 1: **I UNDERSTAND THE USES** of my serger 8
day 2: **I DISCOVER THE ANATOMY** of my serger 14
day 3: **I LEARN WHICH THREADS TO USE** with my serger 20
day 4: **I DISCOVER WHICH NEEDLES** to use 24
day 5: **I LEARN ABOUT** presser feet 28
day 6: **I LEARN TO RECOGNIZE** different fabrics 32
day 7: **I LEARN HOW TO THREAD** my serger 41
day 8: **I LEARN HOW TO ADJUST** thread tension 48
day 9: **I LEARN HOW TO ADJUST** my serger 54
day 10: **I UNDERSTAND** seam allowances 59
day 11: **I LEARN HOW TO MAINTAIN** my serger 61
day 12: **I MASTER** the basic stitches 66
day 13: **I LEARN TO SEW** a corner 74
day 14: **I LEARN HOW TO SERGE** a curve 78
day 15: **I LEARN TO SEW** a rolled hem 83
day 16: **I LEARN TO DO** variations of a rolled hem 88
day 17: **I DISCOVER** the flatlock stitch 92
day 18: **I LEARN TO SEW** an elastic band 95
day 19: **I LEARN HOW TO** gather fabric 100
day 20: **I LEARN HOW TO MAKE** a hem 104
day 21: **I LEARN TO CREATE** stretch waistbands, neckbands, and cuffs 107

bonus

I COMPLETE A PROJECT ON THE SERGER: the Alysa sweatshirt 112
10 QUESTIONS TO ASK YOURSELF when choosing a serger 120
10 THINGS YOU SHOULDN'T DO with a serger 122
5 TIPS for keeping your serger in top condition 124
QUIZ ANSWERS 126
SHOPPING LIST 127

I UNDERSTAND
the uses of my SERGER

day 1

In this book, we're going to talk about the serger in detail. This machine often intimidates beginners, but it becomes truly very easy to use with the right learning method.

THE SERGER: can it replace a sewing machine?

If you are just starting out with sewing and are in the process of getting everything you need, you will undoubtedly wonder whether you can substitute a serger for a sewing machine, in order to save money.

Sergers are quite different from sewing machines. A serger can't replace a sewing machine, but they do complement one another. You should know, however, that your first tool should be the sewing machine.

Sergers are the ideal machine for neatly finishing fabric edges. Even if a sewing machine has specific stitches for finishing edges, the end result won't be very aesthetic. Only a serger lets you achieve the same finish you see on ready-to-wear clothes.

Sergers also have functions for joining fabric pieces, like a sewing machine can. The difference is that the serger allows you to combine two steps in one — construction and serging. Both are achieved in one pass, and much faster than a sewing machine can do.

One doesn't replace the other. **The best option is to have both.**

WHAT MATERIALS can I sew with my serger?

1. woven fabrics

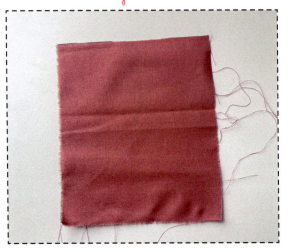

A woven fabric, or one with warp and weft, is made up of interwoven threads. When you cut this type of fabric, little bits of thread come out. So we say this fabric frays. With time, stitches will no longer hold. That's why it's essential to finish the edges. This technique is called serging or overlocking. First you join sections of the work using a sewing machine, then you finish the edges with a serger.

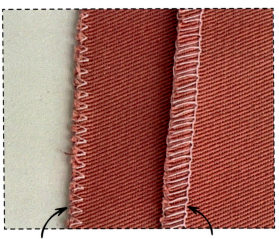

Zigzag   3-thread overlock

It's true that you can also overlock using a sewing machine, in particular with the zigzag stitch, but using a serger gives the finish a much more professional look. As a matter of fact, the serger includes a blade that cuts the fabric while you sew. This allows you to even up the edges of your fabric and achieve a much neater finish.

2. knit fabrics

Knit fabrics, like jersey, are made up of loops. This type of textile has a certain amount of stretch. It is therefore very important to adapt your sewing by using a stitch that can stretch so as to avoid breaking your threads

On some sewing machines, specific stitches let you sew stretch fabrics. However, unlike a sewing machine, a serger allows you to join fabrics while maintaining their elasticity and also finishing the edges. The serger combines two steps in one, and produces a very professional look. This is why it's often said that sergers are ideal for sewing knit fabrics

THE FUNCTIONS of a serger

Sergers have several functions. Let's go over them.

serging

The basic function of a serger is to join pieces and/or serge the edges of your work.

The most commonly used stitch for serging is the 3-thread overlock stitch. It works well for almost any fabric. It can be wide (using only the left needle) or narrow (using only the right).

3-thread narrow overlock

3-thread wide overlock

You can also serge with a 2-thread overlock stitch. This stitch is economical but less sturdy. You may use it for finishing touches or only for delicate fabrics. Like the 3-thread overlock, it can be wide (using only the left needle) or narrow (using only the right).

2-thread narrow overlock   2-thread wide overlock

construction

Sergers allow you to construct projects made of stretch materials, using the 4-thread overlock.

This stitch saves a considerable amount of time, because it joins and serges the edges of knit fabrics in a single step. While you *can* also use it on bulky woven fabrics, or other fabrics with a strong tendency to fray, for these fabrics, it's best not to use the serger to construct and serge at the same time as you would with knits. The end result will not be secure enough.

Bear in mind that if you make a mistake on a serger, it's much harder to fix than on a sewing machine. This is why the sewing machine is better suited for joining woven fabrics

The 2-thread overlock stitch is only used for serging as a finishing touch. This stitch is not strong enough for joining pieces together.

4-thread overlock stitch

{ **NOTE**
The 3-thread overlock stitch can occasionally be used for construction if the fabric is very delicate or very stretchy. }

other functions

Rolled hem

Flatlock stitch

Sewing novices frequently limit themselves to serging with 3 threads and constructing with 4, believing that the serger doesn't offer any other possibilities. However, this machine allows you to do many other things, such as:

Rolled hems:

This is a very close stitch typically used for serging delicate, lightweight fabrics. It can be achieved with two or three spools of thread.

The flatlock stitch:

This is a flat, decorative construction stitch. It has the unique quality of opening the seam and being visible on the exterior as well as the interior of the garment.

Sergers can also be used to create decorative stitches or various sewn works using specific presser feet. In this way, you can attach an elastic band, create gathers, or even make a hem. We'll cover all of this over the course of this book.

· QUIZ ·

Test your knowledge by answering a few questions (answers can be found at the end of the book on page 126).

✘ Can you use the 4-thread overlock stitch on woven fabrics?

✘ What is the name of the stitch frequently used for finishing edges on delicate, lightweight fabrics?

✘ Can you make a hem using a serger?

I DISCOVER
the anatomy of my SERGER

day 2

Now it's time to get to know all about your new machine and its different components.

COMPONENTS SIMILAR
to those of a sewing machine

Sergers have several components similar to those on a sewing machine.

× A **removable presser foot (1)** that lifts using a **lever (2)**.

× A **needle plate (3)**, as well as feed dogs or teeth.

× On some sergers, you may find a **thread cutter (4)**, usually located on the left side of the machine. It's useful for cutting the chain when you're done sewing.

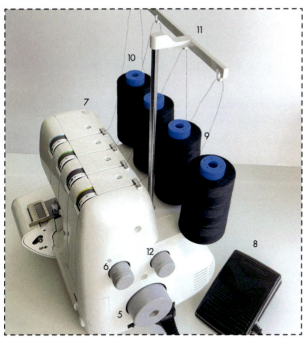

✗ **The handwheel (5)** which lets you raise the needles and manually control the machine in order to sew slowly and precisely.

✗ **The stitch length dial (6)**, allowing you to adjust the distance between needle entry points.

✗ **The presser foot pressure dial (7)** that lets you adjust the pressure to various fabric thicknesses. This adjustment is very important, since the wrong pressure (too weak or too strong) could lead to irregular stitching.

✗ **A power cord and pedal for controlling your sewing speed (8)**.

✗ Some machines also have an extension table to increase your sewing space and allow you to work more comfortably.

✗ The free arm function, as on a sewing machine. This lets you work more easily on tubular seams as with cuffs.

COMPONENTS SPECIFIC to sergers

✗ Sergers are used with thread cones (between 2 and 4 depending on the desired stitch). The 2 cones on the right are for the **loopers (9)** and the 2 on the left are for **the needles (10)**. The lower and upper loopers allow you to create the overlock stitch by knotting the threads from the needles, and the needles stitch through the loops, securing them.

✗ Sergers also have **a telescopic thread pole (11)**, which allows you to keep the threads taut and guide them from the thread holders to the machine while preventing them from getting tangled together.

✗ **The differential feed dial (12)** lets you control the speed of the feed dogs. Depending on your chosen setting, your fabric can become either stretched out or gathered. This adjustment is very useful with stretch fabrics to prevent them from warping while you sew.

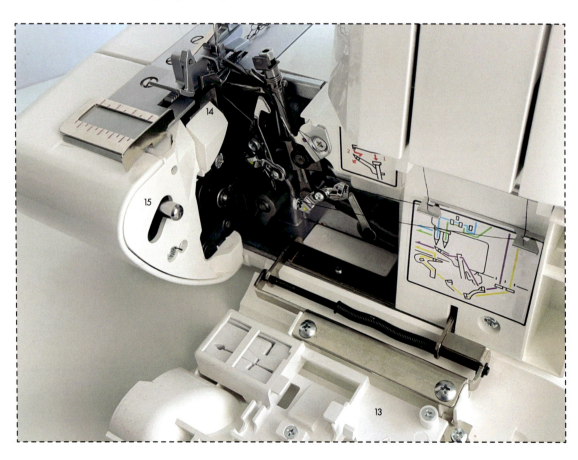

✘ **The front cover of the serger (13)** lowers for direct access to the threading system.

✘ Sergers have a blade located next to **the presser foot (14)**. This lets you remove frayed edges and even up the fabric edges before construction and/or serging steps. When needed, the blade can be disengaged in order to achieve certain stitches (page 57).

✘ Lastly, we have **the cutting width dial (15)**.

✘ Some models have inner compartments for storing certain accessories, such as angled tweezers.

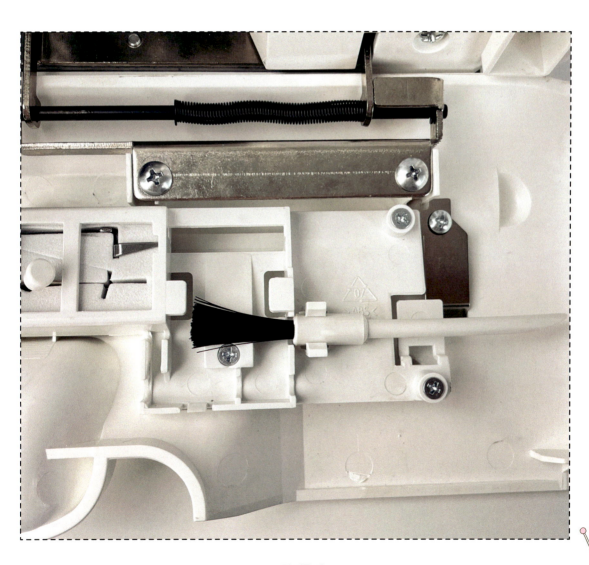

ADDITIONAL ACCESSORIES

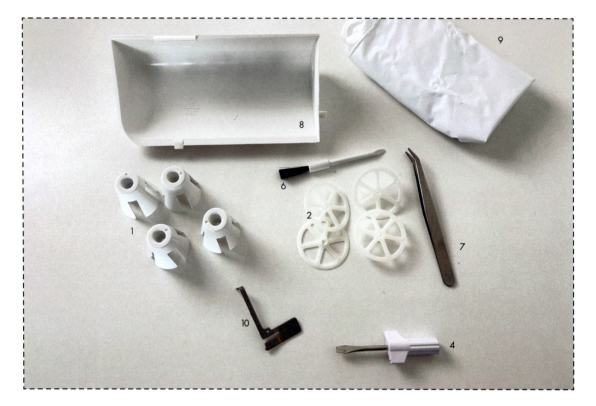

Different accessories typically come with your serger. Among these, you may find:

1. Spool holders. These have different placements on the machine depending on the thread you're using (whether thread cones or traditional spools).
2. Spool caps to hold the spools in place.
3. Thread nets. These allow you to achieve more regular stitches as they ease the unwinding of the thread during the sewing process. Additionally, they prevent the thread from breaking if it's too fragile

4. A screwdriver for changing needles and/or detaching the needle plate.

5. Some sergers have an upper looper converter. This accessory is used to deactivate the upper looper in order to work only with the lower looper and one needle thread.

6. A lint brush for regularly cleaning your serger.

7. A pair of angled tweezers, very helpful when threading.

8. Some serger models have a scrap catcher to catch the extra thread and fabric cut off by the machine. It fits very easily in front of the front cover and allows you to maintain a neat workspace.

9. A protective cover

10. On certain models, you may also have an accessory called a stitch finger. This enables the threads from the upper and lower loopers to remain nice and flat during sewing, and thus lets the fabric roll over onto itself.

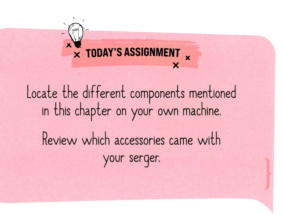

TODAY'S ASSIGNMENT

Locate the different components mentioned in this chapter on your own machine.

Review which accessories came with your serger.

I LEARN WHICH THREADS
to use with my SERGER

Sergers use three or four spools of thread, while sewing machine require only one. Let's dive into their characteristics.

THREAD material

Sergers require a sturdy thread to properly create their stitches, since they operate at a much higher speed than sewing machines. This is why it's necessary to choose polyester thread, known for its durability. You should avoid threads that are too fragile for the machine, such as cotton or silk.

THREAD form and color

Serger spools are sold in cones. This shape is specifically suited to the serger's speed, as the thread comes off the top of the cone. Furthermore, the threads are stronger than traditional sewing machine thread as well as more economical: they hold more thread than traditional spools, an important quality since sergers use up more thread.

Your serger can be threaded with a maximum of 4 spools: two for the needles and two for the loopers. This enables you to achieve a 4-thread overlock stitch.

If instead you want to create a 3-thread overlock, it's also an option to thread only 3 spools (for the left or right needle and two for the loopers).

These cones should be of the same color for a single-color overlock stitch. However, you can use spools of different colors to create more original projects with varied shades of color.

To start out, we recommend purchasing 4 cones in black for dark fabrics and 4 cones in white for light fabrics. These two "universal" colors will allow you to complete the majority of your serging. Later on you can round out your stock with gray, brown, navy, and beige, which go very well with most fabric colors.

> If you want to serge with a specific color and don't have that color in your stock of cones, you can always use a spool of "all-purpose" sewing machine thread.

THREAD size

Unlike with needles, the higher the number on the label, the finer the thread will be. Serger thread comes in several sizes, but the most commonly used is no. 120 or 125, which is appropriate for any type of serging.

RECOGNIZING quality thread

We recommend you invest in high-quality thread from the very start in order to avoid sewing issues while serging. Problems on the serger are more difficult to resolve than those made with the sewing machine, so it's important to choose your thread carefully.

Avoid cheap thread, which may damage your serger and create irregular stitches. Watch out, too, for inexpensive thread cone bundles found in stores that aren't specialized in sewing. The best course is to do your shopping in sewing stores.

Furthermore, take the time to inspect your thread for quality. It should not fray or pill; its surface should be smooth.

The thread should also be very strong. Do a simple test by trying to break the thread between your hands. If it breaks easily, it is not quality thread.

If you have any doubt, trust well-known brands such as Gutermann, Madeira, and Mettler.

Poor-quality thread that pills

Smooth, high-quality thread

SPOTLIGHT ON WOOLY THREAD

Wooly thread is a very strong and stretchy textured thread. It enables your stitches to remain intact when your garment stretches. It is also very soft to the touch.

Because of this, it's especially suited to clothing that will be worn against the skin or for highly elastic fabrics like Lycra. It's therefore preferred for lingerie, undergarments, swimwear, and athleticwear.

Wooly thread comes in both polyester and nylon. Wooly nylon thread is even stretchier and thus the best choice for sewing stretch materials.

Sturdy and textured, wooly thread prevents your stitches from breaking when your garment stretches.

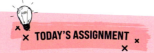

TODAY'S ASSIGNMENT

Add serger thread cones to your shopping list.

· QUIZ ·

Answer the following questions (answers can be found at the end of the book on page 126).

✗ Why does serger thread come in cones?

✗ What size thread is the most commonly used with sergers?

✗ Which thread is best for sewing clothes worn next to the skin?

I DISCOVER which NEEDLES TO USE

Needles are among the serger's most important accessories. Even if you have mastered perfect serging, if you use the wrong needle for the fabric, your stitching may not turn out right

NEEDLE type

There are two categories of needles that work with sergers:

✘ Universal sewing machine needles, with the code 130/705H.

✘ Universal Overlock Serger needles, which you can find with the code ELx705.

Before changing your needle, you'll need to verify in your serger's manual which needles are compatible. If you can't find this information, call the company's customer service.

If your manual advises using only serger needles (ELx705), you should use this type of needle exclusively.

If, on the other hand, your serger can use universal sewing machine needles (130/705H), you can use both serger needles and sewing machine needles.

However, bear in mind that with serger needles, you won't have to change your needle each time you change fabric type. With needles made for traditional sewing machines, on the other hand, you will need to change the needle to suit your fabric and then adjust the tension every time. For example, you would need to use a jersey needle for sewing jersey or a universal needle for cotton. This can quickly become tiresome, which is why we recommend that you buy serger needles from the start.

{ Serger needles also come in a jersey-specific variety. They bear the code ELx705 SUK. These are even better for working with highly elastic materials like Lycra. }

NEEDLE size

Make sure to use the appropriate size needle for your project. A needle with a larger diameter will be less likely to break when working with a thick fabric. On the other hand, it may create large holes in a lightweight fabric.

Each type of needle includes a variety of diameter sizes to allow you to sew different fabric weights. Sizes range from 60 to 120. To choose the best fit for your sewing project, you only need to remember one rule: the higher the number, the better the needle will be for thick fabrics.

For sewing with a serger, we generally use needles sized 80/12 to 90/14.

CHANGING the needle

Before replacing a needle, make sure the machine is turned off. Turn the handwheel counterclockwise until the needle bar is at its highest position while leaving the presser foot lowered.

With one hand, unscrew the needle clamp screw. If your serger has only one screw, hold both needles in your other hand, because once the screw is undone, both needles will fall out. If you have a clamp screw for each needle, unscrew the one that corresponds to the needle you want to change, or unscrew both if you are changing both needles.

Place the new needle(s) into the needle bar with the rounded side facing you, going as far up as possible, then tighten the screw until you feel resistance.

Make sure the needle is straight and securely in place. If you have correctly positioned your needles, the right needle should be slightly lower than the left one.

Unscrew the needle clamp screw with one hand.

Place the new needle(s) in the needle bar with the rounded side facing you.

A TIP FROM MODESTY

{ Be careful! A common mistake is to turn the handwheel either way to raise or lower the needle. However, you should always turn the handwheel toward you, never away! }

TODAY'S ASSIGNMENT

✗ Find out which needles are compatible with your serger.
✗ Check which needles you already have at home.
✗ Add serger needles to your shopping list if necessary.
✗ Learn how to change needles on your serger.

I DISCOVER WHICH NEEDLES TO USE

• QUIZ •

Answer the following questions (answers can be found at the end of the book on page 126).

✗ If my manual recommends using serger needles, can I use ELx705?

✗ True or false? The higher the number, the better the needle is for lightweight fabrics.

✗ For sewing with a serger, what size needle is generally used?

I LEARN about PRESSER FEET

day 5

Like a sewing machine, sergers can use different presser feet depending on what you're sewing. Let's dive in!

THE DIFFERENT presser feet

the all-purpose presser foot

This is the standard foot that comes with your serger and the one you will use most often, as it is used for 3- and 4-thread overlock stitches and for rolled hems.

Other presser feet can be purchased separately and are used specifically for certain sewing techniques. Let's take a look at the most common ones.

the elastic presser foot

This foot is used for sewing elastic bands, which usually come in a width of ¼″ to ½″ (5 to 12mm). Attaching elastic with this tool results in very professional work, since the elastic is uniformly stretched while the fabric edges are serged. If you intend to regularly sew lingerie or swimwear with your serger, I highly recommend investing in this presser foot.

the piping presser foot

Even though attaching piping is a technique often done with a sewing machine, you should know it's also possible to do directly with a serger. The special piping foot combines in one step both attaching the piping and finishing the fabric edges.

This piping foot looks a lot like an all-purpose foot, with one small difference: a groove on the underside of the foot, allowing it to smoothly guide the piping already positioned between the two pieces of fabric.

the blind hem presser foot

The blind hem technique requires the use of a special presser foot, whether on a sewing machine or a serger. This technique creates hems that are barely visible along the edges of skirts and pants.

the gathering presser foot

With the gathering foot, you can gather one piece of fabric while joining it with another piece that remains flat (for example, this is very useful when creating gathers on the bottom part of a dress while joining it with the bodice).

CHANGING the presser foot

Changing the presser foot takes no time at all. Before you begin, make sure that the needle bar is in its highest position.

1. Lift the presser foot lever to raise the foot.
2. Press the release button to remove it.
3. Place your chosen presser foot on the needle plate.
4. Lower presser foot lever and once again press the release to make the holder clamp onto the foot.

1 Raise the presser foot.

2 Press the presser foot release.

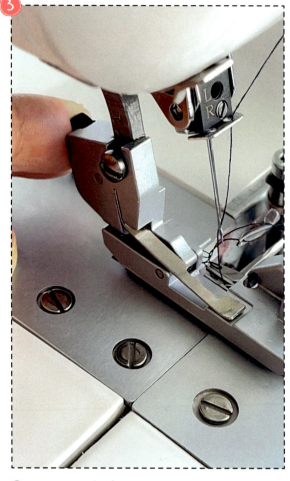

3 Reposition the foot.

TODAY'S ASSIGNMENT

× Add serger presser feet to your shopping list if necessary.
× Practice changing the presser foot.

I LEARN to recognize different FABRICS

day 6

Fabric is the base material for sewing work, and so it is very important to learn to understand it

FIBERS

Before fabric, there is fiber. This fiber is transformed into thread in order to make a textile. There are two main categories of fiber: natural fibers and synthetic fibers.

natural fibers

These fall into two subcategories:

× Animal fibers, such as:

- **Wool:** Comes from sheep fleece. Merinos produce an especially high-quality wool.
- **Cashmere:** This is a high-end fiber that is lighter than wool but also much warmer (up to 8 times warmer than wool).
- **Angora:** This is one of the finest fibers, creating a very soft material that is very nice to wear, with no itchiness. However, this wool tends to thin and pill very quickly.
- **Mohair:** This is a very breathable fiber. It perfectly wicks moisture, keeps cold out in winter, and lets the skin breathe in summer. This wool is distinctive for its shininess. It does not generally lose its shape and is relatively easy to care for.

✎ **Alpaca:** This is a very high-end fiber that is warm, soft, and lighter than sheep's wool.

✎ **Silk:** Silk comes from silkworm cocoons. Silk is cool in summer and warm in winter. This is an expensive and particularly delicate fiber.

× **Plant fibers, such as:**

✎ **Cotton:** This fiber is pleasant to wear but also very absorbent. This fiber tolerates high temperatures well and is therefore easy to care for. However, cotton will wrinkle easily and shrinks substantially in its first few washes.

✎ **Linen:** This fiber is perfect for summer because it barely insulates at all, but it wrinkles even more than cotton.

✎ **Jute, hemp, or even grass cloth:** These are natural fibers that are used less and less frequently these days.

Cotton flowers

Linen flowers

× A TIP FROM MODESTY

{ Be careful: just because a fiber is natural does not mean it's eco-friendly! Cotton farming is among the most polluting forms of agriculture: it requires a great deal of water (the equivalent of 70 showers for a simple t-shirt). }

synthetic fibers

These fall into two subcategories:

✕ **Synthetic fibers made from natural fibers, then transformed via a chemical process, such as:**

- **Viscose:** This fiber was designed to resemble silk as closely as possible. Viscose is a very easy fiber to care for but is also delicate. It does not pill and it falls beautifully. The drawback is that it wrinkles quickly and tends to shrink during its first few washes.
- **Rayon:** This is a stronger fiber than viscose and more absorbent than cotton. It is flexible, soft, and has the advantage of not shrinking. For this reason, it's ideal for making household linens.
- **Lyocell:** Also called Tencel, this is a synthetic fiber whose manufacture is more eco-friendly than viscose or rayon. This fiber is stronger than cotton, but less flexible than viscose.

✕ **Synthetic fibers that are the result of a chemical transformation, such as:**

- **Polyester:** This is the most produced synthetic fiber in the world and the most commonly used. Polyester is sturdy, it dries quickly, and its care is simple. However, it cannot withstand high temperatures, tends to produce static electricity, and pills quickly.
- **Nylon:** Nylon looks a lot like polyester, but it is stronger and more waterproof.
- **Acrylic:** This fiber was created to imitate wool. This fiber has the advantage of being warm and lightweight, but it pills quite fast.
- **Elastane:** Also known as Lycra or Spandex, this is a particularly stretchy fiber. It can stretch up to 7 times its original length and returns to its original shape without deforming. No fabric can be made of 100% elastane. This fiber is added in small quantities to other materials in order to make them stronger, stretchier, and also more comfortable. The higher the percentage of elastane, the stretchier the fabric will be.

 **A TIP FROM MODESTY**

{ Use textiles with mixed fibers to combine the properties of each. For example, a cotton/polyester blend will be more fluid than plain cotton, and cotton containing elastane will be more resistant to damage. }

BONUS

On page 40, you will find a table summarizing the different care instructions for these fabrics.

FROM THREAD to fabric

To transform thread into a textile, there are four methods: weaving, knitting, felting, and lace. Let's spend some time with the two most common:

weaving

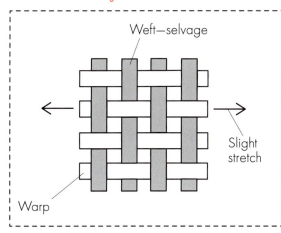

Woven fabrics (fabrics with warp and weft) are fabrics whose threads are woven together on a loom.

In order to create fabrics with different appearances, there are several ways the threads can be interwoven, which is called the weave (plain weave, twill weave, satin weave, velvet weave...). Among the best-known woven fabrics, we can list crêpe, muslin, batiste, gabardine, and even denim.

Spotlight on elastane:

Woven fabrics only stretch in the direction of the bias, or diagonal. To remedy this and make clothing more comfortable, a small percentage of elastane is added to these fabrics. This makes them slightly stretchy and increases their lifespan. Most frequently, a fabric stretches along the weft, or cross grain, perpendicular to the selvage (we call this stretch fabric), but elastane can also be used in both directions (what we call bi-stretch fabric).

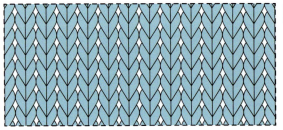

knitting

To understand knit fabrics, simply picture knitting with yarn and needles: links are made by forming interlocking loops.

Industrially, knit fabrics are manufactured using large knitting machines, but the principle remains the same. The links offer a natural stretchiness, but elastane can be also be added. This can counteract the clothing's tendency to deform, but also improve its ability to spring back to its original shape and size. This is particularly useful when it comes to neckbands, which endure a lot of stretching when passing over the head.

THREE ESSENTIAL POINTS TO REMEMBER

✘ Each type of fabric can be made with different fibers. This is how we get cotton jersey, viscose jersey, polyester jersey, as well as cotton viscose, poly-viscose, silk viscose...

✘ Fibers can be mixed together: for example, a cotton/polyester jersey or a linen/cotton gabardine.

✘ Elastane is the ultimate fiber for comfortable clothing worn next to the skin. Its super stretchy power increases fabrics' durability and lifespan.

LET'S LOOK AT SOME KNIT FABRICS in detail

Sergers are generally purchased to make sewing knits easier, so I'd like to delve a little deeper into them in this book. Here is a list of the knit fabrics you'll encounter the most, along with their degree of difficulty, ranging from 1 to 3 stars: 1 star for the easiest fabrics and 3 for the fabrics that are hardest to sew.

jersey (★★)

Jersey is the best-known knit fabric. It is easily recognizable by the little Vs on the wrong side of the fabric and waves on the right side. Cutting jersey can prove tricky because its edges have a tendency to roll.

Jersey can be made from different materials. The easiest to sew is 100% cotton jersey. Its downside is that it doesn't spring back very well: it struggles to regain its shape after being stretched. Look for cotton jersey containing elastane to mitigate this issue. Viscose jersey, on the other hand, is more difficult to sew but the way it falls is second to none. It is perfect for projects that require the fabric to drape beautifully. Last is velvet jersey, which looks like velvet but is a knit fabric. When cutting, it's important to make sure all the pieces are in the same direction, with the pile toward the bottom. It's an ideal fabric for making children's pajamas.

interlock (★)

Interlock is made of two layers of jersey. This makes it stronger and more stable than jersey, and is therefore easier to sew. Its edges do not roll. However, this is not the right fabric if you're looking for something that drapes well.

french terry cloth (★)

Terry cloth is rather easy to sew. It is thicker than jersey but stretches less. The right side of the fabric looks a lot like jersey, but is distinct for the little loops on the wrong side. These loops can be cut to create a warm, soft fleece.

milano knit (★)

This is a knit that is very easy to work with because it doesn't roll. I would go so far as to say that it's the best fabric to start out with when working with knits. Milano holds up better than jersey, which makes it the perfect fabric for dressmaking.

pique knit (★)

This is the fabric used for the famous crocodile brand polos. Pique knit does not roll and is very easy to work with. The difficulty level is close to that of Milano knit.

nylon spandex knit (★★★)

This knit is commonly called Lycra. It contains nylon but also a decent percentage of elastane, which is how it gets its name (Lycra is the commercial name for elastane). This is an ideal fabric for making swimwear, because it dries very quickly. However, it is quite difficult to work with.

> **A TIP FROM MODESTY**
>
> The difficulty levels listed here only correspond to knits. A 100% cotton fabric will obviously be far easier to work with than a 1-star fabric listed above.

TODAY'S ASSIGNMENT

- Go to a fabric store to discover and observe the different textiles discussed in this chapter.
- Make an inventory of your own fabric stock.

A TIP FROM MODESTY

{ To help you get your bearings when it comes to managing your fabrics, download our special fabric stock info cards. You will find them by simply scanning this QR code or going to: tinyurl.com/11630-patterns-download }

MY FABRIC STOCK
Knits

Modesty Couture

GLUE FABRIC SWATCH HERE

Date ....

TYPE ....
FIBER ....
YARDAGE ....
WEIGHT ....
SOURCE ....
PRICE ....

☐ NEEDLE ON HAND ☐ PRE-WASHED
☐ MATCHING THREAD

MY FABRIC STOCK
Woven fabrics

Modesty Couture

GLUE FABRIC SWATCH HERE

Date ....

TYPE ....
FIBER ....
YARDAGE ....
WEIGHT ....
SOURCE ....
PRICE ....

☐ NEEDLE ON HAND ☐ PRE-WASHED
☐ MATCHING THREAD

I LEARN TO RECOGNIZE DIFFERENT FABRICS

FABRIC CARE GUIDE

NAME	WASHING	SPIN CYCLE	DRYING	IRONING	NOTE
LINEN	Machine wash up to 100°F (40°C) or up to 140°F (60°C) for very thick linen).	Gentle spin (600 to 800 rpm maximum) to make ironing easier.	Tumble dry permitted, but line drying is preferred in order to avoid wrinkling the fabric.	With a hot iron, between 400°F and 425°F (200° to 220°C), on still moist fabric.	Try to wash linen with other natural fibers like cotton. Avoid polyester, which leaves lint on the linen fibers.
COTTON	Machine wash up to 100°F (40°C).		Tumble dry permitted at a medium temperature so as not to deform and/or shrink the fibers.	With a hot iron, between 350°F and 400°F (180° to 200°C).	Cotton does well in hot wash cycles, but this is better for household linen and towels. White cotton can be washed as hot as 190°F (90°C) and color cotton as hot as 140°F (60°C).
POLYESTER	Machine wash up to 85°F (30°C).		Tumble dry permitted.	With an iron at medium temperature, 300°F (150°C).	Be aware that athletic wear (and water-resistant materials in general) should not be washed with softener so as to avoid damaging the impermeability.
VISCOSE	Machine wash up to 85°F (30°C).		Do not tumble dry. Air dry only.	With a damp cloth and an iron at low temperature, around 225°F (110°C).	Be aware that viscose has a tendency to become shiny quickly when ironing.
WOOL	Do not wash too frequently, machine wash on a special wool setting or cold wash.	Minimum spin (400 rpm maximum).	Do not tumble dry. Air dry only.	With a damp cloth and a hot iron, 300°F (150°C).	Make sure not to add too much detergent to the machine, as wool tends to pill.
SILK	Machine wash cold on a gentle cycle without softener.	No spin. Press in a towel to gently remove water.	Do not tumble dry. Air dry on a hanger.	Do not iron.	When hand washing, never scrub or over-agitate silk. It's best to use a special wool or silk detergent.

A TIP FROM MODESTY

✗ Think about turning your clothing inside out when washing in order to preserve the fabric's true color and to avoid damaging the fibers.

✗ To limit wrinkling your creations in the wash, don't overfill the machine.

✗ If you accidently stain one of your projects, here are some tips for making it go away:
- Grease stains can be removed with baking soda.
- Blood and grass stains can be removed using gall soap.
- Yellow sweat stains can be removed with white vinegar.
- Coffee, chocolate, or fruit stains can be removed with castile or Marseille soap.

I LEARN how to thread my SERGER
day 7

When you buy your serger, it may already be threaded. If that's the case, you'll need to unthread it completely so you can practice. To do this, cut the threads at the needles and loopers, then pull them to the left while turning the serger's handwheel toward you.

THREADING

To correctly thread your serger, it's essential to follow a specific order. This order varies depending on your model: You need to start by threading either the lower or upper looper. Check your manual to be sure of the correct order for your machine. To help you, sometimes there are numbers to follow directly on the machine itself. For example, if the upper looper is marked with the number 1, that's where you should start.

To make threading easier, every serger also has a color code. Each color corresponds to one thread's path.

For your first time, I recommend threading your machine with 4 spools of thread corresponding to your machine's color coding. Having a different color for each thread will help you better understand the threading, but also help you run the tension tests described in the next chapter.

Once you've mastered threading your machine and tension tests hold no more secrets, you can thread your serger with spools in whatever colors you choose.

Threading precautions: before you start threading, make sure the machine is powered off and the various tensions are set to their minimum (on 0) so the threads are nice and slack. This will prevent the threads from breaking during the threading process. Raise the presser foot to its highest position.

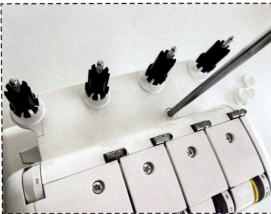

THREADING steps

Pull the telescopic thread pole up to its tallest position.

Position the spool holders, then the spools of thread in their places at the back of the machine.

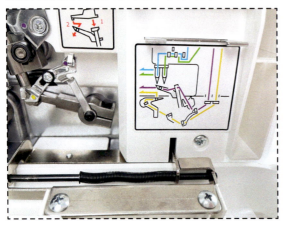

On sergers, you will generally find a diagram on the right side of the machine that summarizes the threading process.

The threading order is often outlined inside the serger.

THREADING the upper looper

Pass the upper looper thread (second spool from the right; here, the purple thread) through the eyelet on the telescopic thread pole from the back to the front. Pull the thread about 6˝ (15cm) **(photo 1)**.

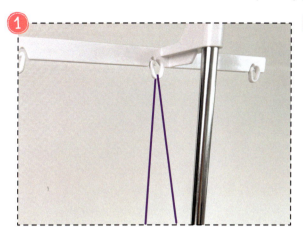

Pass the thread through the hook located in front of the spool and slide it through the tension disc **(photo 2)**.

Next, follow the numerical order for the upper looper color coding, passing the thread around the corresponding hooks **(photo 3)**.

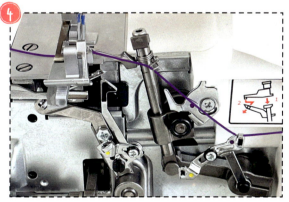

Pass the thread through the eye of the upper looper using the tweezers, then pull it to the left to position it under the presser foot **(photo 4)**.

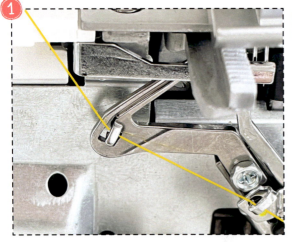

THREADING
the lower looper

Pass the lower looper thread (the spool farthest on the right; here, the yellow thread) through the eyelet on the telescopic thread pole from the back to the front. Pull the thread about 6″ (15cm).

Pass the thread through the hook located in front of the spool and slide it through the tension disc.

Next, follow the numerical order for the lower looper color coding, passing the thread around the corresponding hooks **(photos 1–3)**. Pass the thread through the eye of the lower looper using the tweezers and bring the threads over to the left.

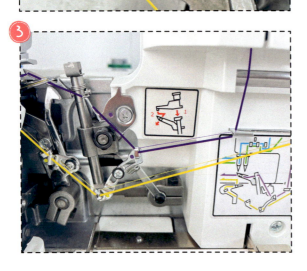

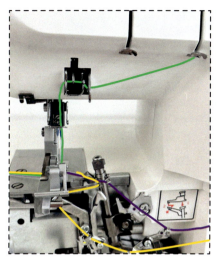

THE RIGHT needle

Pass the right needle thread (the spool third from the right; here, the green thread) through the eyelet on the telescopic thread pole from the back to the front. Pull the thread about 6˝ (15cm).

Next, follow the numerical order for the right needle color coding, passing the thread around the corresponding hooks. Pass the thread through the eye of the right needle using the tweezers, then pull it to the left to position it under the presser foot.

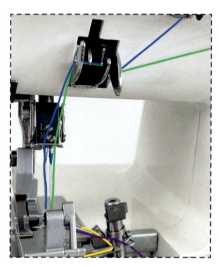

THE LEFT needle

Pass the left needle thread (the spool farthest on the left; here, the blue thread) through the eyelet on the telescopic thread pole from the back to the front. Pull the thread about 6˝ (15cm).

Next, follow the numerical order for the left needle color coding, passing the thread around the corresponding hooks. Pass the thread through the eye of the left needle using the tweezers, then pull it to the left to position it under the presser foot.

You should have your 4 threads on the left and should feel no resistance if you pull on them.

• FREQUENTLY ASKED QUESTIONS ABOUT THREADING •

✗ My machine is threaded with only 3 spools and I need to do a 4-thread overlock. Do I need to completely rethread the machine?

No. You just have to add the missing needle, thread it, press the pedal, and generally a chain will form with 4 threads. To go back to a 3-thread overlock, simply remove the fourth spool for the right or left needle and re-form the chain.

✗ I want to make a 3-thread overlock. Do I need to remove the left needle?

Yes, you need to remove the needle or else you will have holes in your fabric and irregular stitching.

THE STITCH TEST

Once threading is complete, turn the machine on, lower the presser foot, and hold your threads with your left hand, gently pulling them toward the back. Turn the handwheel toward you a few times to make sure the threads interweave correctly.

If the machine is correctly threaded, links will form to create what we call the thread **chain**.

Once this step is completed, return the tension dials to their default settings. This setting is usually underlined on the dial. Raise the presser foot and place a piece of medium-weight cotton fabric beneath it.

Some sergers have a guideline so you know exactly where to correctly position the edge of the fabric. If not, position the fabric edge against the edge of the stitch plate.

The fabric should be positioned well below the stitching so it will be cut correctly.

Lower the presser foot, place the thread chain to the back and make a first overlock stitch by gently pressing the pedal. Sew a few stitches, then pull the fabric out to the left.

Finish by making several stitches without fabric for about 6″ (15cm), then cut the threads, leaving about 4″ (10cm) of chain.

CHANGING THREADS the easy way

To easily change threads without having to completely rethread the machine, there is a simple technique called the knotting technique.

how it's done

With the machine turned off, cut the thread of each spool right in front of the thread pole eyelets, then remove the spools **(photo 1)**.

Set all the thread tensions to 0 and raise the presser foot. Place the new spools on their holders and tie each thread to the remaining tails of the previous threads **(photo 2)**.

Once the knots are tied, clip the ends to avoid any tangling of threads. But don't cut them too short, or you risk the threads breaking during rethreading.

Turn the handwheel toward you to pull the threads down. Make sure that each knot correctly passes through each eyelet **(photo 3)**.

For the needle threads, turn the handwheel until just before they reach the eyes of the needles and cut (as the knots may not be able to pass through the eye).

Rethread the needles **(photo 4)**.

Once all the threads have passed through, return the thread tensions to their default settings, make a chain and a stitch test on a scrap of fabric.

TODAY'S ASSIGNMENT

× Thread your machine with spools in colors corresponding to your machines' color coding.
× Make a stitch test.

I LEARN
how to adjust THREAD TENSION

day 8

Just like with a sewing machine, adjusting tension consists of tightening or loosening the sewing thread.

THREAD tension

The lower the tension, the more slack your thread will be. Tension that is too low will result in a very loose and weak stitch. *Conversely*, the higher the tension, the tighter the thread. Tension that is too high will gather the fabric and may cause your thread to break while sewing.

To balance the tensions of your different threads, the serger has dials marked with numbers. Each dial allows you to adjust the tension of each thread individually.

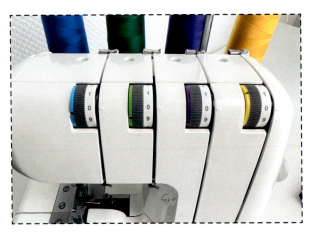

Each dial is marked from 0 to 9, 0 representing the lowest tension and 9 the highest. You may also have simple + and - signs. Each thread also has a preset tension—i.e., a default tension. Generally this setting is between 4 and 5.

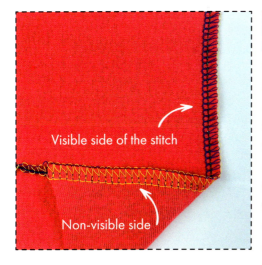

Visible side of the stitch

Non-visible side

CORRECT tension

On a well-balanced overlock stitch, the upper looper thread (purple in the photo) covers the entire edge of the fabric's top side (the side facing you while you sew) and the lower looper thread (yellow in the photo) covers the entire edge of the fabric's underside (the side against the stitch plate during sewing). The right needle thread (green in the photo) runs through the middle of the upper looper thread. The left needle thread (blue in the photo) runs along the left edge of the stitch.

The needle stitches are like a sewing machine's straight stitch: they should be parallel, the same size, and uniformly spaced. They are the same on the right side and wrong side of the fabric.

To help you get the correct tension, your serger's manual will typically include a table with recommended tension settings depending on the desired stitch and the fabric you're using. These suggested settings work very well most of the time, but at times they may not be exactly right and require a few adjustments.

This is why it's imperative that you know how to recognize which thread is responsible if you encounter a problem—and there's no better way to learn than running tests!

The best way to practice is to thread your machine with 4 spools of different colors to easily distinguish which thread is which and quickly determine which one is causing the problem.

Two points of clarification for your tests:

We always start from the default settings and then make adjustments. To do this, make sure you've correctly positioned each thread's tension dial on the neutral number, then increase or decrease the tension as needed.

Only adjust one tension setting at a time, going from right to left. First adjust the upper looper thread tension (here, the purple thread); once it is correct, move on to the lower looper (here, the yellow thread) and so forth. If you try to adjust all thread tensions in one go, you'll struggle to understand which thread is the issue.

> **✗ A TIP FROM MODESTY ✗**
>
> Nylon thread nets may come with your serger. These help hold your thread spools in place and enable them to unwind at the right speed. I recommend putting them on your spools as a precaution, or if you can't achieve a nice stitch.

UNBALANCED tensions

Here are some examples of unbalanced thread tensions.

Loose upper looper thread

problems with the upper looper

Reminder: here, the upper looper thread is purple.

The upper looper thread is too loose

On the top side of the fabric, the upper looper thread (purple) is a little loose. The space between each loop is more spaced out.

On the underside, it goes over the edge although it shouldn't. Meanwhile, the lower looper thread (yellow) doesn't cover the entire space.

We can conclude that the upper looper thread is too loose. We therefore need to increase this thread's tension.

Tight upper looper thread

The upper looper thread is too tight

The lower looper thread (yellow) has come over the upper edge of the fabric, although it should not be visible from this side.

problems with the lower looper

Reminder: here, the lower looper thread is yellow.

The lower looper thread is too loose

On the top side of the fabric, the upper looper thread (purple) is too short: it does not cover the entire space of the fabric edge, and the lower looper thread (yellow) comes over into this area when it shouldn't be seen.

On the underside, we see that the space between each loop of the lower looper thread (yellow) is too wide and that these loops are much too loose; they come apart very easily.

The lower looper thread is too tight

On the top side, we don't see much difference, but on the underside, we barely see any of the lower looper thread. The upper looper thread has come over the edge.

problems with the needle threads

The right needle thread is too loose

Reminder: here, the right needle thread is green.

On the top side, the stitch is too loose. It is not as tight as a normal stitch should be. On the underside, the right needle thread is very loose and forms obvious loops.

The left needle thread is too loose

Reminder: here, the left needle thread is blue.

On the top side, we see that the leftmost stitch is very loose: it's not a regular stitch. On the underside, we don't have tight little stitches but very loose stitches that form little triangles.

Loose lower looper thread

Tight lower looper thread

Loose right needle thread

Loose left needle thread

Tight needle thread

The needle thread is too tight

If the needle thread tensions are too high, your fabric will form deep gathers during and after serging. It will be difficult to feed the fabric through and the thread may break during sewing. If this happens, you will need to decrease the tension in the needle threads.

A TIP FROM MODESTY

Take advantage of the fact that your machine is threaded with 4 different colors of thread to run as many tension tests as possible! Grab a few scraps of several different kinds of fabric (those you work with the most, for example) and practice until you get the perfect tension on each of them. Write down the combinations you get on the data sheet you'll find by scanning this QR code or going to: tinyurl.com/11630-patterns-download

This way, you'll know at a glance how to adjust your serger for each fabric change (see opposite page)!

TODAY'S ASSIGNMENT

× Print the special tensions data sheet.
× Make tension tests for your fabrics.
× Write down the right settings on your sheet.

TENSION SETTINGS
for my Serger

SERGER MODEL: ....

STITCH TYPE: ....   STITCH TYPE: ....
FABRIC TYPE: ....   FABRIC TYPE: ....

TENSION SETTINGS

GLUE FABRIC SWATCH HERE

- LOWER LOOPER ☐
- UPPER LOOPER ☐
- RIGHT NEEDLE ☐
- LEFT NEEDLE ☐

TENSION SETTINGS

GLUE FABRIC SWATCH HERE

- LOWER LOOPER ☐
- UPPER LOOPER ☐
- RIGHT NEEDLE ☐
- LEFT NEEDLE ☐

STITCH TYPE: ....   STITCH TYPE: ....
FABRIC TYPE: ....   FABRIC TYPE: ....

TENSION SETTINGS

GLUE FABRIC SWATCH HERE

- LOWER LOOPER ☐
- UPPER LOOPER ☐
- RIGHT NEEDLE ☐
- LEFT NEEDLE ☐

TENSION SETTINGS

GLUE FABRIC SWATCH HERE

- LOWER LOOPER ☐
- UPPER LOOPER ☐
- RIGHT NEEDLE ☐
- LEFT NEEDLE ☐

Modesty Couture

MODESTY COUTURE • ALL RIGHTS RESERVED

I LEARN HOW TO ADJUST THREAD TENSION

I LEARN
how to adjust my SERGER

One of the values of the serger, but also one of its complexities, is the option of making a ton of adjustments, depending on which fabrics you're working with. It's important to learn about all of these possible adjustments before embarking on a project

PRESSER FOOT pressure

Presser foot pressure refers to the force that the presser foot puts on the fabric while you're sewing.

Sergers generally come already set to a standard pressure that works for most serging. However, certain fabrics require this pressure to be adjusted in order to achieve regular stitches.

This is the case for bulky or very lightweight fabrics.

For bulky fabrics, presser foot pressure needs to be increased to properly compress all the layers. Conversely, for very lightweight fabrics, we need less pressure in order to avoid wrinkling the fabric during sewing.

If you need to adjust this setting, turn the presser foot pressure dial to a higher number to increase pressure or to a lower number to decrease it.

DIFFERENTIAL FEED

Despite its somewhat complicated name, its function is very simple. This allows you to avoid gathering the fabric while sewing. This applies especially to very lightweight fabrics or very stretchy fabrics like jersey. The differential feed dial lets you alter the speed of the feed dogs.

Sergers have two sets of feed dogs (front and rear) which carry the fabric along during serging. If the differential feed dial is on 1 (neutral position), the feed dogs move at the same speed. This default setting is used when not sewing lightweight or stretchy fabrics. This is for basic fabrics, denim, or very thick fabric.

However, it is possible to have different speeds for each set of feed dogs by using differential feed.

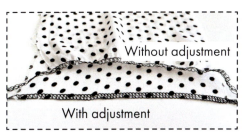

for lightweight fabrics

If you're working with a lightweight fabric, decrease the differential feed setting (lower than 1). With this setting, the front feed dogs move slower than the rear ones. This prevents unwanted gathers from forming.

for stretchy fabrics

If you're working with a stretchy fabric like jersey, you must instead choose a higher setting (greater than 1). The front feed dogs will move faster than the rear ones.

DIFFERENTIAL SETTING	EFFECT ON THE FABRIC	GOAL	FABRIC TYPE
0.7–1	Stretched fabric	Prevent lightweight fabrics from gathering	Lightweight fabrics
1	No effect	Normal stitching	Woven fabrics
1–2	Gathered fabric	Prevent stretchy fabrics from gathering or warping	Stretch fabrics

In any situation, before you begin sewing, it's best to make a few tests on scraps of the fabric you want to sew in order to determine which differential setting works best.

STITCH length and width

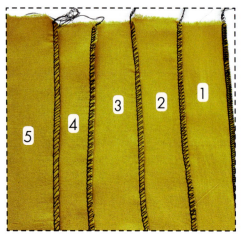

Stitches of different lengths

stitch length

Stitch length is the distance between two of the needle's entry points, exactly like on a sewing machine. The higher the number selected, the longer the stitch. On a serger, we generally leave this setting on its default value. However, for a bulky fabric, stitch length should be increased, and for a lightweight fabric, it should be decreased.

In general, stitch length is adjustable between 1 and 7mm.

stitch width

Stitch width is the distance between the leftmost needle stitch and the edge of the fabric.

This width depends on the number of needles you're using.

If you're using the left needle, meaning you're making a 4-thread overlock or a 3-thread wide overlock, the stitch width can be from 5 to 7mm.

If you're only using the right needle, as for a 3-thread narrow overlock, you will have a lower width setting: stitch width will be between 3 and 5mm.

These values may be different depending on the model you use, so I encourage you to check in your manual which stitch width settings are available.

For a bulky fabric, we typically choose a greater width. Conversely, we opt for a narrower stitch for lightweight fabrics.

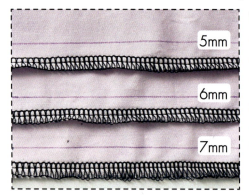

5mm, 6mm, and 7mm overlocks

ENGAGING/DISENGAGING the knife

On this model, the knife is disengaged by pressing a button.

A serger's default setting is to have the knife engaged in order to achieve neat edges. You can, however, disengage the knife, for example when sewing a delicate section as there's too much risk of going off course.

It's also helpful to disengage the knife if you need to join up with the beginning of your seam (tubular sewing, for example), to attach without cutting those first stitches.

How to disengage the knife depends on your serger. Some models let you engage/disengage the knife by simply pressing a button, while others require you to open the front cover and flip a lever.

Learn to engage and disengage your machine's knife by practicing on scraps of fabric.

Don't hesitate to make some stitch tests with and without the knife to get an idea of the results!

> **TODAY'S ASSIGNMENT**
>
> × Make differential feed tests.
> × Test out different stitch lengths.
> × Test out different stitch widths.
> × Try sewing with the knife disengaged.

Serger settings
CHECKLIST

01	CHOOSE NEEDLES AND THREAD	☐
02	THREAD THE SERGER	☐
03	CHECK PRESSER FOOT PRESSURE	☐
04	ENGAGE / DISENGAGE THE KNIFE	☐
05	CHECK STITCH WIDTH	☐
06	CHECK STITCH LENGTH	☐
07	ADJUST THREAD TENSION	☐
08	CHECK DIFFERENTIAL FEED	☐
09	CHECK IF YOU NEED TO ADD/REMOVE CERTAIN ACCESSORIES FOR THE DESIRED STITCH	☐
10	MAKE A STITCH TEST	☐

Modesty Couture

MODESTY COUTURE • ALL RIGHTS RESERVED

I UNDERSTAND
SEAM ALLOWANCES

Seam allowances refer to the amount you need to leave along the fabric's edge to serge safely. To figure out this amount, two measurements should be taken into account: stitch width and cutting width.

As a reminder, stitch width is the width between the leftmost needle stitch and the edge where the knife cuts. It measures between 3 and 7mm according to the desired stitch (page 56).

As for the cutting width, a serger's knife typically cuts between 1 and 2mm of fabric (a value that may vary depending on serger model).

Here's a simple little equation to memorize to help get your bearings:

SEAM ALLOWANCE = STITCH WIDTH + CUTTING WIDTH

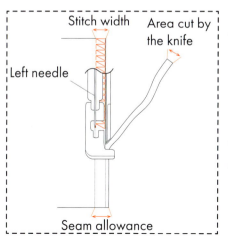

For example, if I choose to sew a 4-thread overlock with a width of 5mm, which I sew while lining the fabric edge up with my stitch plate, cutting off 2mm, I will have a seam allowance of 7mm or ¼″ to complete my serging.

Note: If you disengage the knife, only take stitch width into account to know how much seam allowance is needed for serging.

SEAM ALLOWANCES
for serging projects constructed on a sewing machine

should you serge before or after assembling pieces on a sewing machine?

If you're using a serger to finish the edges of your work, you don't have to calculate seam allowances, given that during construction you already left sufficient seam allowance when tracing your pattern onto the fabric (generally between ⅜″ and ⅝″ or 1 and 1.5cm for construction seams, and around 1¼″ or 3cm for hems). Therefore you simply need to line your fabric up with the edge of the stitch plate and begin serging.

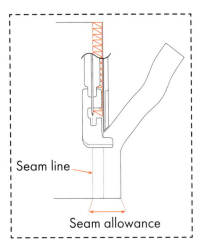

SEAM ALLOWANCES
for constructing on the serger

Seam allowances are especially important to take into consideration if you're using your serger to assemble your project.

It's the left needle that will stitch your seam line. You therefore need to know where to position your fabric according to the alignment between your seam and the leftmost needle. Based on where you position your fabric with respect to this line, it may be that more material will be cut off as you sew.

On certain machines, guidelines help you correctly position the edge of your fabric.

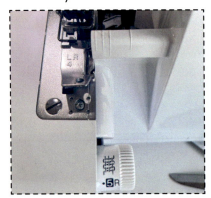

Serger with seam allowance markings

NOTE

In general, leaving ⅜″ (1cm) of seam allowance is enough to serge safely, but run some tests beforehand on scraps of fabric to be sure of your allowances, just in case.

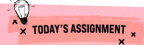

TODAY'S ASSIGNMENT

× Cut some pieces of fabric and try to sew along different guidelines on your serger to better understand seam allowances.

I LEARN
how to maintain my SERGER

day 11

Maintaining your serger is essential for prolonging its lifespan. In this chapter, you'll learn the routine to follow to keep your machine running smoothly for a long time.

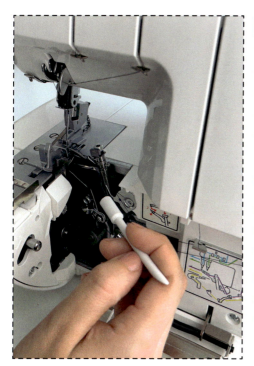

Remove the dust and lint using the brush that comes with your serger.

CLEANING

The first thing to do is to regularly clean your machine. The knife produces scraps of fabric with each sewing. The more you let these scraps accumulate, the more likely they are to stick to components of the machine and contribute to its wear.

Ideally, it should be cleaned after each use.

Before you start cleaning, turn off the machine, then open the front cover as well as the work table. Lift the presser foot.

Using the brush that typically comes with the machine, remove the dust and lint that has built up, taking care to sweep it all forward.

For anything you can't reach with your brush, you can use a compressed air duster (sold for dusting computer equipment).

Lastly, give it a quick vacuum to collect any scraps that have fallen to the bottom of the machine during brushing.

Use a compressed air duster to remove the last scraps and lint.

OILING

With each use, your serger's metallic components rub against each other, which is why it's necessary to oil regularly. This lets the machine work more quietly, last longer, and jam less.

You will need to refer to your serger's manual to be sure you can proceed correctly and know exactly where you should apply the oil to your machine.

Be aware that if you make a mistake as to how much or where to apply the oil, it can lead to serious consequences.

To oil your machine, you will need a bottle of oil, a soft microfiber cloth, and one or two pieces of scrap fabric as well as a small brush (optional).

Use only high-quality sewing machine oil purchased from a sewing store. A poor-quality oil may dry to form a crust that damages your machine as well as the quality of your stitching.

This may sound silly, but I want to clarify: Never use cooking oil or motor oil!

Oil the metallic components with sewing machine oil once your serger is perfectly clean.

Only oil your machine if it's perfectly clean. Just like for cleaning, first turn off your machine and open the front cover. Oiling generally happens around the loopers' metal bars. You should apply oil to a strategic point either on the upper and lower looper or on the upper looper's metal bar. To oil your machine, apply the oil directly or use a small oil brush, which ensures you don't get oil everywhere and can achieve a much more precise application. **Apply one or two drops, but no more.** It's important not to slather the mechanisms in oil. Then turn the handwheel toward you, just to raise and lower the needles to spread the oil around. Close the cover. To avoid getting any oil on your sewing work, make a normal overlock stitch on your scraps of fabric. Any potential leftover oil will be transferred to the scraps and not onto your projects. To finish, wipe down the serger's plastic surfaces with a soft cloth to make sure there are no traces of oil.

MATERIALS and additional accessories

Remember to also check the state of your materials and accessories. Always make sure that any accessories you purchase are compatible with your machine before using them.

• FREQUENTLY ASKED QUESTIONS ABOUT OILING •

✗ **Why do we oil sergers?**

Like any mechanical material, the metal pieces rub against each other, which is why you need to lubricate these components regularly. This way, your serger will run more quietly and last longer.

✗ **Is it necessary to oil your serger?**

Before any intervention, read your manual to make sure your model needs to be oiled.

✗ **How often should a serger be oiled?**

For best results, we recommend regular oiling, about every 20 hours of sewing time. As it can be difficult to estimate your sewing time in hours, I would say every 2 or 3 months is enough for moderate use.

✗ **Is there a special serger oil?**

No. We use the same oil for both sewing machines and sergers.

THE PROTECTIVE cover

Remember to cover your serger with the provided cover when you're not using it, to protect it from any dust that may get into the tension discs and seriously damage your machine in the long term. If your machine didn't come with a protective cover, a simple piece of fabric will work.

The protective cover protects the serger from dust.

REPLACING the upper knife

If your knife gets dull and no longer properly cuts the fabric, you need to replace it.

The lower, fixed knife should only be touched by a professional, or you may damage the machine.

Only the upper, removable knife can be replaced by you, but be careful: Don't attempt this procedure unless you are truly sure of yourself. Incorrectly replacing the knife can mess up your stitching. If you aren't completely sure, call on a professional to change the upper knife.

A TIP FROM MODESTY

{ If you think you can change the knife on your own, take pictures BEFORE you start unscrewing. This will help you ensure the correct positioning afterward! }

POSSIBLE PROBLEMS
during sewing & their solutions

The thread breaks during sewing.

Possible causes:

The thread. If your thread is fragile, try putting the nets on your spools and test. Remember also to check your thread size (as a reminder, a thinner thread is better suited to a lightweight fabric).

If nothing works, change your brand of thread. Don't forget to favor well-known brands.

The threading. Make sure that each thread is in its proper path and that no thread is caught at any eyelet, hook, or spool.

The needles. The tip of a needle may be curved, dull, damaged, or improperly inserted.

The tension. Check that you have the correct tension. Too much tension will break the thread. If this happens, decrease the tension to sew correctly.

the needle breaks during sewing.

The most frequent cause is that the needle is not inserted deep enough into the needle clamp.

The solution is to completely unscrew the needle and then reinsert it correctly. If the issue persists, change your needle, as it may be from a lower quality brand, or you may be using a needle whose size or function is not suited to your serger and/or fabric. Verify in your manual which needles you should use with your serger.

To improve the lifespan of your needles, avoid pulling too hard on your fabric behind the presser foot while you sew, as this can cause your needles to become deformed over time.

the fabric edge continues to fray after serging.

This is a problem with the knife. Either it's not engaged, or it needs to be changed.

First change the upper knife, test it out, then change the lower knife.

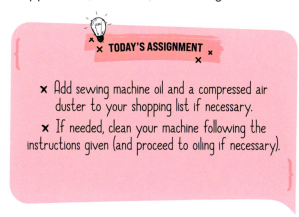

TODAY'S ASSIGNMENT

× Add sewing machine oil and a compressed air duster to your shopping list if necessary.
× If needed, clean your machine following the instructions given (and proceed to oiling if necessary).

I MASTER the BASIC STITCHES

day 12

We've covered all the adjustments you need to make in order to sew under the best conditions. We can now finally move on to practical application.

SEWING precautions

Before diving in, here are a few precautions to take, which will make your sewing easier.

The first thing, as we've seen already in this course but as a reminder, you never know, is to make a chain of an inch or two before beginning to sew.

Also make sure that the needles and presser foot are both raised before positioning your fabric, and don't forget to lower the foot before starting up the machine.

If you hold your fabric in place with pins, place them parallel to the fabric's edge—vertically, not horizontally. The serger moves the fabric very quickly, so if you place your pins horizontally, you run the risk of their being pulled into the machine's mechanism and damaging your stitches or even your machine. Furthermore, you will see that placing your pins parallel to the edge will enable you to remove them more easily as you progress. Make sure to place them far enough away from the edge to minimize the risk of sewing into them.

Place the pins parallel to the fabric's edge.

Clips are ideal for holding fabric.

You can also use little clips, which are even more convenient to remove and cause less damage to lightweight fabrics.

Another option is to baste (basting consists of pre-stitching by hand to hold the two fabrics together), to run the least risk possible.

> **A TIP FROM MODESTY**
>
> Stitches made with a serger are harder to remove than those of a sewing machine. I therefore recommend you always start on the most delicate side of your project, as it's easier to correctly position your work at the beginning of a seam than at the end.

SERGING

As we covered when introducing the serger's functions, you can make a 2- or 3-thread overlock.

how do you serge?

The 3-thread overlock stitch

This is the stitch most commonly used for serging. It suits pretty much all fabrics. It can be narrow (around 3mm) when working with only the right needle, or wide (between 5 and 7mm on average) when only using the left needle.

The 3-thread narrow overlock stitch

The 3-thread narrow overlock stitch

Adjustments:

Remove the left needle, then adjust your serger according to the instructions found in your manual regarding tensions and stitch width. If necessary, adjust the tension.

Position the edge of your fabric against the edge of the stitch plate. Lower the presser foot and press down on your pedal to start sewing.

Don't forget to sew a few stitches without fabric at the end of your seam to make the chain.

Good to know: When working with only one needle thread, you may be tempted to be lazy and simply unthread the needle you don't need instead of removing it. This is something you should never do: otherwise, loops will form beyond the edge and your stitches won't have any regularity. You will also get holes in your fabric. So always remove the needle you're not using before you sew!

The 3-thread wide overlock stitch

For the 3-thread wide overlock, follow the same process as for the 3-thread narrow overlock, but remove the right needle instead.

The 3-thread wide overlock stitch

The 2-thread overlock stitch

Put the converter on the upper looper.

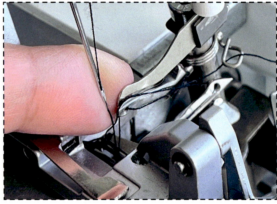

This enables you to deactivate the upper looper.

This stitch is economical, but not very sturdy. You may use this as a finishing touch and only on lightweight fabrics. When making a 2-thread overlock, the serger sews with only one needle thread (right for a narrow overlock or left for a wider overlock) and the lower looper thread. You need to put the converter accessory on the upper looper in order to deactivate it.

Caution: Once you've finished and don't need to make any more 2-thread overlocks for the time being, don't forget to remove the converter.

CONSTRUCTION

The serger allows you to join stretch fabrics. To do this, you need to use the 4-thread overlock stitch. This saves considerable time, as assembling and serging the edges of knit fabrics happen in a single step.

For construction, position your fabric pieces one against the other, right sides together.

To make this overlock stitch, follow the same procedure for the 3-thread overlock but using both needles. The 4-thread overlock stitch is accomplished by using both serger needles and both loopers. The result is a stitch at once flexible and strong.

The 4-thread overlock allows you to assemble and serge in a single step.

SECURING
and undoing stitches

securing your stitches

On a serger, there is no stop stitch like on a sewing machine, but you still need to secure your stitches so they don't come undone over time.

To do this, you have the choice of several techniques.

✗ Securing with a needle

Make a chain of around 4˝ (10cm), then take a large-eyed needle and slide it under the sewing threads for about 1˝ (2 to 3cm).

Thread the needle with the end of your chain and pull it through to the other side. You can now safely cut off the remaining chain.

Thread the chain through the eye of the needle.

Draw the chain under the stitches for about 1˝.

Pull the needle through.

Cut the remaining chain.

Your seam is secure.

✖ **Securing with glue**

You can secure the stitches with fabric glue. To do this, put a dot of fabric glue on the end, then cut the chain short.

A dot of fabric glue also lets you secure your seam.

✖ **Securing by continuing your chain on the other side**

At the end of your stitches, don't make a chain but instead stop at the edge of your fabric. Next, raise your presser foot and turn your fabric over, then lower the presser foot again. Stitch for 1˝ (2 or 3cm), pulling your fabric to the left so the knife doesn't cut your stitches. Cut the chain short.

At the end of your seam, stop at the fabric's edge.

Raise the presser foot and turn the fabric over.

Lower the presser foot and complete a few stitches.

Cut the chain short.

Your seam is secure.

UNDOING YOUR OVERLOCKS

To undo stitches you've sewn, cut the needle thread(s) at regular intervals using a pair of embroidery scissors and remove the looper threads.

Cut the needle thread(s) at regular intervals.

Pull out the looper threads.

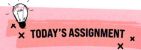

TODAY'S ASSIGNMENT

× Make a 3-thread overlock in both wide and narrow widths.
× Make a 2-thread overlock in both wide and narrow widths.
× Make a 4-thread overlock.
× Secure your seams, trying out the different techniques listed.
× Undo a seam.

I LEARN to sew A CORNER

day 13

You'll quickly find yourself faced with sewing a corner, whether exterior or interior. This technique is relatively simple to learn, but it does require a little practice.

SEWING an exterior right angle

Knowing how to sew a nice exterior angle on a serger is useful for finishing a rectangular piece.

Start by serging the first side, then raise the presser foot and remove the fabric. Cut the chain at the edge of the fabric. There's no need to secure the seam here, as we will create a second seam over the first.

Place your fabric back under the presser foot, positioning it 90° from the previous seam. Lower the presser foot and serge the edge perpendicular to the previously serged edge. This second overlock with cover the beginning of the first.

1 Serge the first side.

2 Serge the second side.

3 You now have a perfect corner.

SEWING
an interior right angle

It can be useful to know how to create a nice interior right angle, especially when making clothing (necklines or the edges of facing, for example).

Start by making a ⅛″ notch (3mm) in the interior corner using a pair of embroidery scissors, then position the fabric and begin serging normally. At the notched corner, raise the presser foot and open the corner, pulling on the fabric so that the seam line is straight. Lower the presser foot and serge in a straight line over the corner. Use an iron to completely flatten the right angle.

1 Make a notch in the interior corner.

2 Flatten the fabric toward the left so as to obtain a straight seam.

3 Serge in a straight line over the corner.

4 You now have a perfect interior corner.

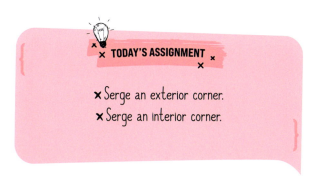

TODAY'S ASSIGNMENT

× Serge an exterior corner.
× Serge an interior corner.

day 14
I LEARN to serge A CURVE

The technique of serging curves is largely the work of your hands: They will guide the fabric so that the serger takes the curve correctly.

SERGING an interior curve

The left hand pushes the fabric toward the left and the right hand toward the right as you serge. The curve must remain parallel to the edge of the serger's stitch plate.

1 Your hands guide the fabric so that the curve remains parallel to the edge of the stitch plate.

2 You now have a perfect interior curve.

SERGING
an exterior curve

The right hand pushes the fabric toward the left and the left hand toward the right. The curve must follow the edge of the serger's stitch plate, so you have to pull it back and push the edge of the fabric against the edge of the plate.

1 Your hands guide the fabric so that the curve remains parallel to the edge of the stitch plate.

2 You now have a perfect exterior curve.

A TIP FROM MODESTY

Whatever the type of curve, the stitches should be as regular as possible. Guide the fabric slowly to maintain control of the stitches.
Take care that the fabric doesn't slip under the knife while you sew.

SEWING a circle

Sewing a circle follows the same principle as the exterior curve: You just have to follow the shape of a circle as you serge and make sure that the fabric's edge always stays lined up with the edge of the stitch plate.

When your sewing is complete, you will need to disengage the knife to secure the thread by going back over the first stitches for about ¼″.

1 To sew a circle, follow the shape of the curve and make sure that the edge of your fabric always stays lined up with the edge of the stitch plate.

SERGING a tube

To properly finish your seam at the end of a tube, you need to carefully overlap your starting and ending stitches. Line up the edge of your first stitches with the edge of the presser foot to sew over the seam and not to the side. Cut the chain and disengage the knife.

Make a few stitches manually over the first stitches by turning the handwheel toward yourself. Help the serger to draw your fabric along by gently pulling it from the back.

To make sure you've sewn over the entire missing section, you can raise the presser foot while leaving the needles in the fabric. Check that you've sewn the entire edge.

Lower the presser foot again, then pull your fabric while sewing a few stitches without fabric to create your chain.

You can now cut the chain short, given that your stitches are secured by the connection of the two serged seams.

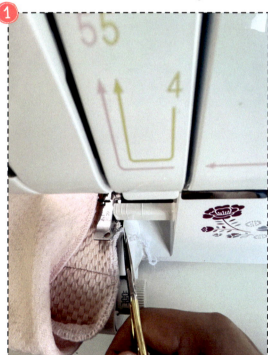

1 Cut the chain.

2 Make a few stitches manually over the first stitches by turning the handwheel toward yourself.

3 Raise the presser foot, leaving the needles still inserted in the fabric, to make sure you've sewn across the entire missing section.

4 Cut the chain short.

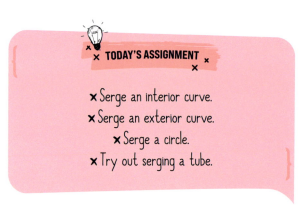

TODAY'S ASSIGNMENT

× Serge an interior curve.
× Serge an exterior curve.
× Serge a circle.
× Try out serging a tube.

I LEARN to sew a ROLLED HEM

day 15

The rolled hem, also called a pin hem, is a finishing stitch that makes a very narrow fold wrapped in thread along the edge of the fabric.

WHICH FABRICS?

You can do a rolled hem on lightweight or very lightweight, woven or stretch fabrics. For example, you can do this with cotton voile, silk, linen, crêpe, satin, or lightweight jersey. With these kinds of fabric, it can prove difficult to sew a standard hem, so the best method is to go for a rolled hem, if you want to finish your work neatly and easily.

ADJUSTMENTS

This stitch requires only the right needle and can be done with either 3 or 2 threads.

For the best possible result, you should use a fine needle: size 80 or, for midweight fabrics, size 90.

You can use basic polyester thread, or you can use wooly thread (which covers more) or metallic thread (for a decorative effect).

As for threading the right needle and loopers, thread your machine and leave it threaded as you normally would.

Follow the instructions in your manual to know how to set your serger.

On some machines, you'll need to remove the accessory called the stitch finger. In the chapter on the anatomy of the serger, we discussed how the stitch finger makes it so the upper and lower looper threads remain flat while you sew. It therefore prevents the fabric from rolling up onto itself. However, since this is precisely what we need to create our rolled hem, we need to disengage it (refer to your manual to find out how this is done).

The 3-thread rolled hem is very tight. It's ideal for a visible finish along fabric edges

the 3-thread rolled hem

Once your serger is properly adjusted, position your fabric under the presser foot with the right side of the fabric facing you. This way, when you've finished sewing, the fold will form on the back of the fabric and not on the front.

the 2-thread rolled hem

For a 2-thread rolled hem, the serger only sews with the right needle thread and the lower looper thread. You will need to put the converter on the upper looper to deactivate it (page 68).

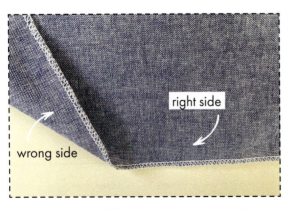

The "narrow hem" finish lets you achieve a hem without folding the fabric over.

the 3-thread overlock stitch

To add a delicate, elegant finish or to join two pieces of stretch fabric, there's also the 3-thread overlock stitch, called a narrow hem. Unlike the rolled hem, you achieve a flat finish without folding the fabric onto the wrong side.

The settings for this stitch are typically detailed in your serger's manual.

the rolled hem in a tube

To create a rolled hem, follow the same procedure as for tubular serging (page 81).

Sew your rolled hem, then to neatly finish your stitches, line up the edge of your first stitches with the edge of the presser foot to sew over these stitches and not off to the side. Cut the chain and disengage the knife.

Serge manually over the first few stitches by turning the handwheel toward yourself. Help the serger to draw the fabric through by gently pulling from the back.

To make sure that you have indeed sewn over the entire missing section, you can raise the presser foot while leaving the needles in the fabric. Check that you've sewn along the entire edge.

Lower the presser foot again, then pull your fabric while sewing a few stitches without fabric to create your chain.

Line up the edge of your first few stitches with the edge of the presser foot.

Sew over the stitches.

Cut the chain short.

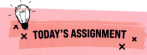

TODAY'S ASSIGNMENT

✗ Make a 3-thread rolled hem.
✗ Make a 2-thread rolled hem.
✗ Make a 3-thread narrow hem.

I LEARN to do VARIATIONS OF A ROLLED HEM

day 16

The rolled hem can be reimagined with more creative variations.

THE LETTUCE HEM

The lettuce or frilled hem is a rolled hem that creates little waves. To achieve this result, set the serger as you would for a standard rolled hem and stretch the fabric as you sew, or increase the differential feed.

Generally speaking, the more you increase the differential feed, the more pronounced the wavy effect will be, but the result also depends on the fabric's elasticity. Don't hesitate to make some tests on scraps before working on your final project.

The lettuce hem undulates more or less depending on your chosen fabric and settings.

PINTUCKS

These are decorative folds that you can make on the right side of a project. They can be achieved with a 3-thread rolled hem.

how it's done

Draw straight, parallel lines on the right side of the garment, where you want to sew the pintucks. The length of the folds and the space between them is entirely up to you.

Create a fold on the first line, wrong sides together, and iron.

Make new lines at the beginning and end of this fold with an erasable pen.

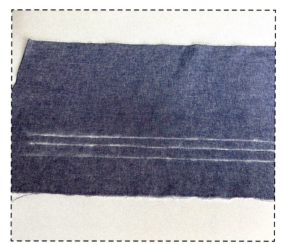

Draw straight, parallel lines on the right side of the garment.

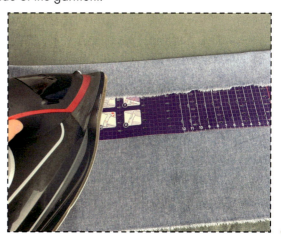

Create a fold on the first line and iron.

Disengage the knife (page 57) and sew all along this fold on the right side of the fabric with a 3-thread rolled hem, starting at the beginning line you've just drawn.

Sew all along this fold with a 3-thread rolled hem.

Just before you finish these stitches, lower the needle, raise the presser foot, pivot the fabric to the left, lower the presser foot, then pull the fabric out.

To secure these stitches, thread the chain through a large-eyed needle and sew into your fabric to pull it through on the wrong side.

Cut this thread, leaving about ½" or 1cm.

Use an iron to flatten the pintuck in the direction you want.

Repeat these steps for each pintuck.

Repeat these steps for however many pintucks you want.

TODAY'S ASSIGNMENT

× Make a lettuce hem.
× Make some pintucks.

I DISCOVER the FLATLOCK STITCH

day 17

The flatlock stitch is a flat stitch that creates a looping stitch on one side of the garment and a series of bars that resemble a ladder on the other side.

It is reversible. The unusual thing about the flatlock stitch is that once the serging is complete, you gently pull on the seam with your hands to make the threads appear.

The flatlock stitch on the right side of the fabric

The flatlock stitch on the wrong side of the fabric

WHICH FABRICS

You can use this stitch on any kind of fabric, whether woven or stretch, lightweight or bulky.

ADJUSTMENTS

It's up to you whether you want to work with the left needle for a wider stitch or with the right needle if you prefer a narrower stitch.

tension settings

To do this stitch, you need to work with a very low tension in the needle thread, i.e. zero. The upper looper has a medium tension, 5, and the lower looper has a high tension, 8 or 9. This allows you to stretch the stitch without encountering any resistance.

stitch length

The stitch length should be set between 2 and 3mm and the other settings are similar to those of a basic overlock stitch.

> **NOTE**
> The flatlock stitch is not a stitch that your serger makes on its own. It is created simply by manipulating the tensions of the needle thread and lower looper.

THE RESULT

With this reversible stitch, you have two options:

If you want the loops on the wrong side of the fabric and the ladders on the right side, position the fabric with right sides together and the wrong side facing you while you sew.

If you want the loops on the right side of the fabric and the ladders on the wrong side, sew with the wrong sides together and the right side facing you.

THE FLATLOCK STITCH
for construction

To join two pieces of fabric together: Position them wrong sides together or right sides together—depending on your desired result—and serge.

Once the seam is complete, pull the two pieces of fabric to open the stitches and create the flatlock stitch.

Pull the two pieces of fabric and open the stitches to create the flatlock stitch.

TODAY'S ASSIGNMENT

× Make a flatlock stitch.

I LEARN
to sew an ELASTIC BAND

You can use this technique when sewing different covers, like a fitted sheet or an ironing board cover, or to add elastic bands to clothing. The width of the elastic band you should use depends on the presser foot you have. Generally, they run from ¼" to ½" (5 to 12mm) wide.

To sew an elastic band, you have 2 options::

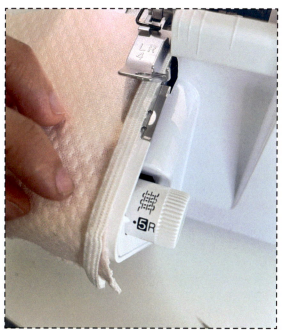

✗ Simply position the elastic band along the edge of the fabric and stretch the elastic while you serge. This method is a little difficult to do, as it requires some dexterity to correctly place the elastic band and not slip during serging.

Though a delicate process, it is possible to sew an elastic band without a special presser foot.

Using a special presser foot makes attaching elastic easier.

✗ Using the elastic presser foot helps you properly hold the elastic band in place while sewing and makes sure you maintain the same tension for the entire seam.

To use this special foot, you need to slide the elastic band into the slot on the foot. Then increase the pressure on the elastic band using a dedicated dial or screw. The elastic band will thus be held in place during sewing and will be joined directly to the fabric.

The higher the tension on the elastic band, the more your elastic will be stretched. In this case, the fabric will be tightly gathered.

Conversely, if you want slacker elastic and less gathered fabric, choose a lower tension.

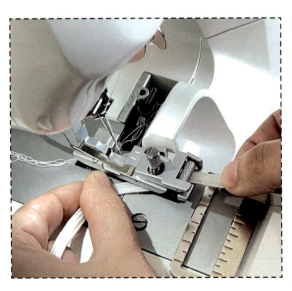

Slide the elastic into the slot on the special presser foot, then adjust the tension on the elastic band using the dial or screw.

STEPS
for adding an elastic band with the special elastic presser foot

To easily insert the elastic into the presser foot, decrease the tension on the dial to 0. Once the elastic is in place, tighten the screw or turn up the dial to the desired tension.

Next, position the elastic presser foot.

Adjust the tensions on your serger to suit your fabric and lower the presser foot. Sew a few stitches without the fabric to make sure the elastic band is pulled through the foot while sewing.

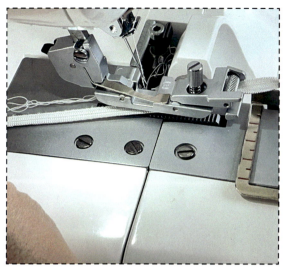

Raise the presser foot and then position your fabric beneath the foot, lining up its edge with the edge of the elastic band (the fabric's edge should be parallel to the elastic's edge above it). Serge while holding the elastic with your hand so that it stays straight and is correctly pulled throughout your sewing.

I recommend making a few tests on your fabric, adjusting the presser foot's tension to see how it affects the result.

Sew a few stitches without fabric to make sure that the elastic band is pulled through by the presser foot.

With these different tests, you'll be able to determine how much your fabric will gather so you can sew the elastic band perfectly onto your final project.

To add elastic to two pieces of fabric at the same time, follow the same principle as described above. The only difference is that you need to place the fabric wrong sides together and line up the two fabrics' edges before starting your seam.

Place the fabric under the presser foot, edge to edge with the elastic band.

Result on the right side

Result on the wrong side

Adding elastic while joining two pieces of fabric

SEWING A TUBE
with elastic

To sew an elastic band on the end of a tubular section and neatly finish your seam, line up the edge of the first stitches with the edge of the presser foot to sew over the seam and not off to the side. Cut the chain and disengage the knife.

Make a few stitches manually over the first stitches by turning the handwheel toward yourself. Help the serger draw the fabric through by gently pulling from the back.

To make sure you have indeed sewn the entire missing section, you can raise the presser foot while the needles remain in the fabric. Check that you've sewn the entire edge.

Lower the presser foot once more, then pull the fabric out while sewing a few stitches without fabric to make your chain.

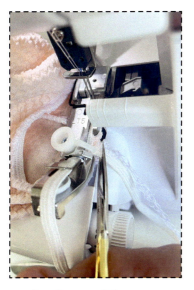 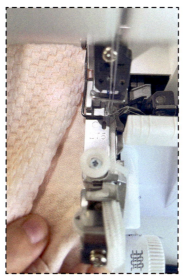 

Cut the chain and disengage the knife.

Make a few stitches manually over the first stitches by turning the handwheel toward yourself.

Make your chain and cut the elastic band.

TODAY'S ASSIGNMENT

× Attach an elastic band.

I LEARN how to GATHER FABRIC

day 19

Sergers let you gather fabric in a number of ways.

GATHERING ONE PIECE of fabric

Using a serger to gather one piece of fabric is simple: All you need to do is set the differential feed to its maximum value and increase the stitch length, whether for woven or stretch fabrics. As a reminder, the differential feed dial allows you to control the speed of the feed dogs. Depending on your chosen setting, your fabric either stretches or gathers. See Day 9 (page 55).

Maximum differential feed and increased stitch length allow you to easily achieve gathers.

CONSTRUCTION and gathering

If you want to assemble your pieces and gather at the same time (for example, if you want to create a sleeve with frills), you have two options:

× Gather one piece of fabric first, using the technique described above, then position the gathered and non-gathered fabric right sides together under the all-purpose presser foot and serge the edges together.

× Use the gathering presser foot with two pieces of non-gathered fabric. This allows you to achieve both steps in one.

The gathering presser foot allows you to gather one of two fabric pieces while you serge.

gathering presser foot technique

Thanks to the gathering foot, one of the two pieces of fabric will be gathered as you sew while the other fabric remains flat.

Position the first piece of fabric under the presser foot with the right side facing you. This piece will be gathered and cut during serging.

The fabric onto which you'll be attaching the gathered piece will be placed in the slot on the presser foot with the wrong side facing you. This fabric will remain flat as you sew. Line up the edges of your two fabrics, placing the two ends on top of one another.

Place the first piece of fabric with the right side facing you.

Place the second piece of fabric in the presser foot's slot, wrong side facing you.

Thanks to the gathering foot, the first fabric is gathered during sewing, while the other remains flat.

> **A TIP FROM MODESTY**
>
> For even more pronounced gathers, increase the needle thread tension.

GATHERING ratio

When you gather fabric, it bunches up, so naturally you'll lose material. To avoid ending up with two pieces of fabric that are not the same length once joined, you need to make a little calculation, what we'll call the gathering ratio.

To do this, take a fabric scrap with a given length, gather it with the serger, and measure how much length was lost.

For example, if you start with a 12″-long piece of fabric and after gathering it only measures 6″ long, you need to plan for twice as much fabric for your gathering (12/6 = 2).

If you start with a 12″-long piece of fabric and after gathering it only measures 8″ long, you will need 1.5 times as much fabric for gathering (12/8 = 1.5).

This ratio will vary depending on what fabric you use. Some fabrics gather more than others. This is especially the case for very lightweight fabrics.

The best thing to do is to make tests with the fabric you plan to gather and calculate the gathering ratio. You will take this value into account when tracing your patterns and cutting your fabric.

> **NOTE**
>
> If you're worried you can't calculate the gathering ratio accurately enough, you can always make your gathers in two steps using the all-purpose presser foot. Then it's easy to adjust the length of the gathered fabric by gently pulling on the needle threads.

In any case, bear in mind that you will always need more fabric when gathering. So remember to run your tests beforehand to know how long of a piece you need to cut for the pattern, because even with the first gathering technique, you need to try to get as close to the gathering ratio as possible. It can actually be quite difficult to alter a lot of gathers by pulling on the threads—even more so given the risk of breaking the threads.

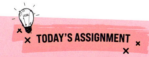

TODAY'S ASSIGNMENT

✗ Make gathers without the gathering presser foot.
✗ Make gathers with the gathering presser foot.

I LEARN how to make a HEM

You can make a hem directly on your serger. Though it can be done with woven fabrics, this is even more suited to knit projects.

HOW IT'S DONE

Put the right side of the fabric facing you.

Fold the fabric's edge, wrong sides together, according to the desired hem width. For example, for a 1″ hem, fold the edge back 1″.

Flip the fabric over and make a new fold with right sides together. You will have a sort of accordion fold.

Iron the folds and pin or clip to hold in place.

Fold the edge of the fabric, wrong sides together, depending on your desired hem.

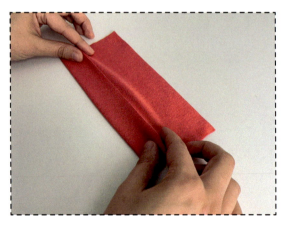

Flip the fabric, then fold again, right sides together.

Adjust your serger according to the fabric you're using.

Sew the edge, lining up the fabric's edge with the presser foot (you are therefore sewing through three layers at the same time).

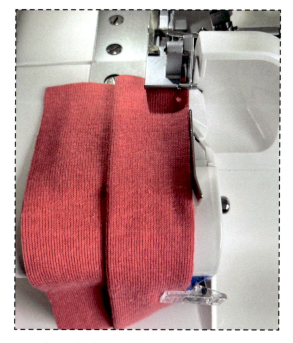

Sew through all three layers, lining up the fabric edge with the presser foot.

Once you've finished stitching, press the hem.

You now have a perfect hem.

Finish by topstitching with a twin needle on a sewing machine to flatten the hem.

Topstitching with a sewing machine allows you to flatten the hem.

TODAY'S ASSIGNMENT

× Make a simple hem.

I LEARN
to create STRETCH WAISTBANDS, NECKBANDS, AND CUFFS

We use stretch bands to neatly finish neckbands, cuffs, or the bottom edges of a garment (if it has a waistband or ankle cuffs).

To make these stretch bands, you can simply cut them from the cloth you're using to make your garment (if the fabric has at least some elasticity) or you can buy fabric specifically designed for this purpose, called jersey rib knit.

CALCULATING neckbands

calculating neckband width

Before attaching the neckband, it will need to be folded in half lengthwise, so you need to plan for twice the desired final width.

Example: for a final width of 1″, make sure to have an initial width of 2″. Don't forget to also add the top and bottom seam allowances you'll need for construction.

calculating neckband length

Measure the circumference of the neckline, either directly on your pattern or on the already assembled garment.

Measure the fabric's elasticity. To do this, cut a piece of fabric perpendicular to the selvage, i.e. the direction in which it has the most stretch.

Mark both ends of a given interval, for example 4″. Stretch the fabric as far as you can and make a note of the new length.

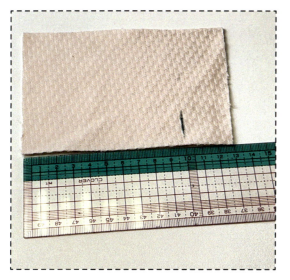

Mark out 4″ on your fabric.

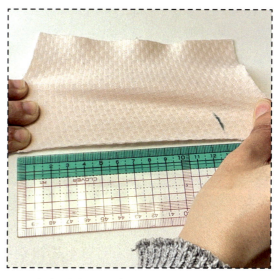

Stretch the fabric as far as you can and make a note of the new length.

Then make this calculation:

(length of stretched fabric/length of unstretched fabric - 1) ×100 = stretch percentage

Or

(stretched length - initial length)/initial length × 100 = stretch percentage

Multiply the circumference of your project's neckline by the multiplier corresponding to your fabric's stretch percentage as presented in the table below:

	NECKBAND			
FABRIC STRETCH PERCENTAGE	<50%	50%	80–100%	100% or more
MULTIPLIER	0.85	0.8	0.75	0.7

To this amount, add the left and right seam allowances needed for construction. Now you have the length of your neckband.

Example:

Neckline circumference: 22″ with a stretch percentage of 50%, so: 22 × 0.8 = 17.6.

Don't forget to add the right and left seam allowances needed for constructing the neckband.

CALCULATING cuffs and waistbands

For these stretch bands, choose a width greater than that of your neckband for a well-balanced result.

calculating the band's width

Follow the same procedure as for the neckband: each of these bands will need to be folded in half lengthwise so always plan for twice the desired final width.

Calculating the band's length

Follow the same procedure as for the neckband:

Measure the circumference of the cuff and/or bottom edge of the garment, either on the garment itself or from the pattern

Measure your fabric's elasticity (as explained for the neckband). Multiply this amount by the multiplier corresponding to your fabric's stretch percentage as presented in the table below:

	CUFFS AND WAISTBAND	
FABRIC STRETCH PERCENTAGE	Stretch between 30 and 50%	Stretch greater than 50%
MULTIPLIER	0.9	0.85

> **NOTE**
> We explain how to sew these bands in the Alysa sweatshirt pattern tutorial in the bonus portion of this book (page 117).

I COMPLETE a project ON THE SERGER: THE ALYSA SWEATSHIRT

To reinforce all that you've learned throughout this book, we recommend making a project that can be made entirely on a serger. A sweatshirt is a great first project! There are many sweatshirt patterns available. If you'd like to try ours, you can download the Alysa sweatshirt and follow along here.

PATTERN AVAILABLE FOR SIZES 4–14 (36–46 IN EUROPEAN SIZING).

The Alysa sweatshirt is a knit base that offers a wide range of possibilities for personalization: adding a rib knit, creating cut-outs or patches, adding a gathered frill, etc. Let your imagination run wild!

MATERIALS

✘ Around 1²⁄₃ yards (150cm) of knit fabric, 60″ wide (150cm)
✘ Optional: ¾–1 yard (70–100cm) of jersey rib knit depending on your size, 12″ wide (30cm)
✘ You can also use your main fabric instead of rib knit

Full-size downloads of the patterns are available at:

tinyurl.com/11630-patterns-download

ACCESSING PATTERNS

✘ To access the pattern through the tiny url, type the web address provided into your browser window.

✘ To access the pattern through the QR code, open the camera app on your phone, aim the camera at the QR code, and click the link that pops up on the screen.

TIPS

To sew the Alysa pattern, it's absolutely essential to choose a knit fabric. Here is a list of fabrics that will definitely work for this project:

✘ Sweatshirt fabric
✘ Fleece
✘ Quilted jersey

If this is your first sweatshirt, avoid fabrics with a strong tendency to roll or fabrics that are too bulky.
Before sewing, remember to wash your fabric and carefully iron it.

PRINTING AND ASSEMBLING THE PATTERN

If you can, print from Adobe Acrobat Reader.

Print page 3 of the pattern, choosing the "actual size" option, and check the dimensions of the 1″ scale or 10cm test square.

If the dimensions are correct, print the rest of the sheets on US Letter-size paper.

Cut one of the two page borders and join the pieces together with tape, making sure to properly match the lines of the final piece.

Example: Mark P. 1 should line up with page 1, mark P. 2 should line up with page 2, and so on.

A summary of pattern assembly is available on the first page of the PDF pattern.

Sizing guide

SIZES	4 (36)	6 (38)	8 (40)	10 (42)	12 (44)	14 (46)
BUST	30″–31″ (76–79cm)	31½″–34″ (80–87cm)	34½″ × 37½″ (88–95cm)	38″–40½″ (96–103cm)	41″–43″ (104–109cm)	45″ (110cm)
WAIST	23½″–24½″ (60–62cm)	25″–27″ (63–68cm)	27″–29½″ (69–75cm)	30″–32½″ (76–83cm)	33″–35″ (84–89cm)	35½″ (90cm)
HIP	34″–35″ (87–89cm)	35½″–37½″ (90–95cm)	38″–40″ (96–101cm)	40″–43″ (102–109cm)	43″–45″ (110–114cm)	45″ (115cm)

CUTTING INSTRUCTIONS

The Alysa PDF pattern is made up of 3 pieces:

- ✗ **1 front:** cut 1 on the fold
- ✗ **1 back:** cut 1 on the fold
- ✗ **1 sleeve:** cut 2

In addition to these pieces, you need to cut the following bands:

- ✗ Cut 1 neckband on the fold
- ✗ Cut 2 cuffs
- ✗ Cut 1 waistband on the fold

See the table below for the dimensions of these bands, but be aware, these measurements are given only as a guide.

To achieve the best possible results, your dimensions should take your fabric's stretch percentage into account. To create high-quality bands, follow the instructions on page 107.

Neckband, cuff, and waistband measurements

SIZES	4 (36)	6 (38)	8 (40)	10 (42)	12 (44)	14 (46)
NECKBAND	16⅛″ × 2″ (41 × 5cm)	16½″ × 2″ (42 × 5cm)	17⅜″ × 2″ (44 × 5cm)	17¾″ × 2″ (45 × 5cm)	18⅛″ × 2″ (46 × 5cm)	18½″ × 2″ (47 × 5cm)
CUFFS	7⅛″ × 3⅛″ (18 × 8cm)	7½″ × 3⅛″ (19 × 8cm)	7⅞″ × 3⅛″ (20 × 8cm)	8⅝″ × 3⅛″ (22 × 8cm)	9″ × 3⅛″ (23 × 8cm)	9½″ × 3⅛″ (24 × 8cm)
WAISTBAND	26⅜″ × 4″ (67 × 10cm)	28¾″ × 4″ (73 × 10cm)	3½″ × 4″ (80 × 10cm)	33⅞″ × 4″ (86 × 10cm)	35⅜″ × 4″ (90 × 10cm)	37⅜″ × 4″ (95 × 10cm)

SEAM ALLOWANCES

The Alysa pattern does not include seam allowances. We recommend adding ¼″ to ⅜″ (0.7 to 1cm) for your seam allowances.

Plan larger seam allowances if your fabric rolls a lot in order to make sewing easier.

If your fabric is difficult to mark, add these seam allowances around all the pattern pieces. This will allow you to cut out your fabric by following the edge of the paper.

Optional: You can adapt this sweatshirt by making a hem at the bottom (instead of adding a waistband). In this case, tack on an additional 1¼″ (3cm) for the hem.

CUTTING LAYOUT

The Alysa sweatshirt is cut out in two steps:

✗ Fold your fabric with right sides together, placing the selvages edge to edge so as to create two folds, and cut out the front and back pieces.

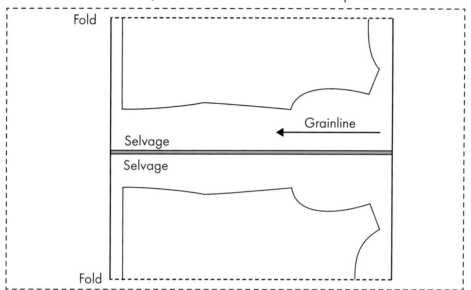

✗ Then fold your fabric right sides together, this time placing the selvages one on top of the other, and cut out the remaining pieces: the sleeves and cuffs as close as possible to the selvage; the neckband and waistband on the fold.

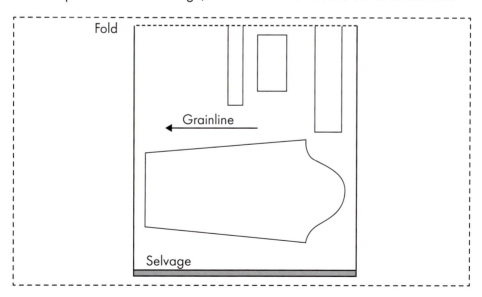

> **NOTE**
> Depending on the chosen size, the cutting layout may be adjusted.

SEWING STEPS

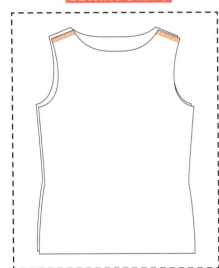

step 1: joining the shoulder seams

Position the front and back right sides together and pin at the shoulders.

Sew these seams using the 4-thread overlock stitch.

Press the seams open.

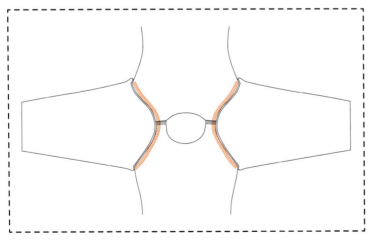

step 2: joining the sleeves

Sew each sleeve to each armhole, right sides together.

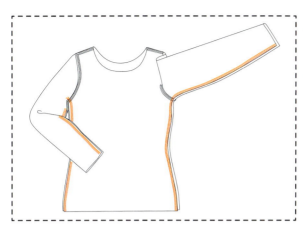

step 3: closing the sides

Close one of the sleeves and the corresponding side of the sweatshirt with pins (or by basting if needed).

Serge the entire seam and repeat on the other side.

step 4: joining the stretch bands

Gather the neckband, cuffs, and waistband you've cut for your sweatshirt.

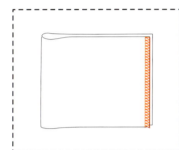
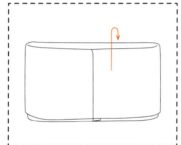

Preparing the bands:

Close each band to form a circle, joining its ends with right sides together. Fold it in half lengthwise with wrong sides together and iron to crease.

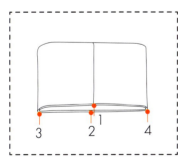

Divide each band into fourths:

Place a pin along the seam and another on the opposite side.

Lay these pins one on top of the other and place a third and fourth pin at each end.

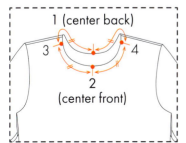

Divide the garment into fourths:

For the neckline: mark and pin the center back and center front. Position these two pins one on top of the other and place a third and fourth pin on each side to mark out fourths.

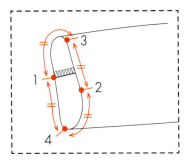

For the sleeve openings:

Mark and pin the seam and the opposite side. Position these two pins one on top of the other and place a third and fourth pin on each side to mark out fourths.

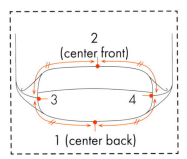

For the bottom of the sweatshirt:

If your back and front have the same length, follow the same procedure as you did for the sleeve openings. If there is a difference between the two, follow the same procedure as you did for the neckline, first marking the center back and center front before the opposite sides.

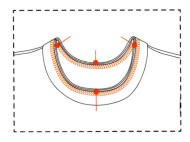

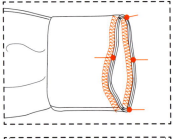

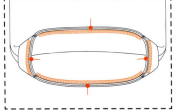

Attaching the neckband, cuffs, and waistband:

Match the pins on the band with those on the garment, right sides together, lining up the raw edges.

Place the fabric with the right side facing you and sew an inch or two on the serger to secure the 3 layers. Start at the center back for the neckband and at the seam for the other bands.

Sew, pulling the materials and proceeding quarter by quarter so that the band is properly stretched and lines up perfectly with the correct section of the garment. Before you get back to the starting chain, disengage the knife and sew over the first few stitches for ¼″ or so.

Raise the presser foot, pull the sweatshirt backward, then lower the foot and sew without fabric to form your chain.

Topstitch on the machine and sew ⅛″ (3mm) from the edge to prevent the band from flipping over.

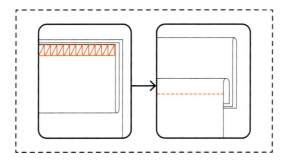

Your sweatshirt is complete. Bravo!

10 QUESTIONS TO ASK yourself WHEN CHOOSING A SERGER

QUESTION #1:
Do I need a serger?

Many people say that sergers are unnecessary and there are plenty of alternatives for making those professional-looking final touches, such as the zigzag stitch, the flat felled seam, or the French seam. However, the result will never be as neat as with a serger. In any situation, it will require a lot more time and a lot more work without a serger. The serger becomes an inevitable purchase if you sew regularly and if you want to achieve a well-made final project.

QUESTION #2:
What types of stitches do I want to sew?

Every serger has 4 spools and can make the 2- or 3-thread overlock, the 2- or 3-thread rolled hem, the 4-thread construction (overlock) stitch, and the flatlock stitch. We generally use the 4-thread overlock for construction and the 3-thread overlock for finishing. So it's not really the number of available stitches on a serger that should influence your purchase. On the contrary, the two criteria to take into account are the ease of changing the stitch and the ability to achieve a good result. Adjusting the machine may differ and be more or less tedious depending on the model. Before you buy, you need to see if you can easily juggle the different adjustments. If you spend too much time readjusting the serger each time you change stitches or fabric, it may discourage you from using it.

QUESTION #3:
Is it easy to thread?

Threading is another point to check, as it's often what creates the most problems. It may seem somewhat complex, but its degree of difficulty varies from one model to the next. On some sergers, it can be a real struggle, but on others, it's child's play. There are sergers with automatic threading and with automatic tension adjustments as well, but these are much more expensive than those with manual adjustments. If at all possible, you should find a machine that will cause you the least amount of problems in this critical process of threading. The best course is to look for reviews or online videos to get a glimpse into what you can expect.

QUESTION #4:
Which adjustments are available?

Several adjustments are very important. To begin with, there's differential feed. Make sure that this is available on your serger. Also check if it has a good range of stitch lengths and widths so you have plenty of options for your stitching. You should also see if your serger's knife can be disengaged. During sewing, the serger cuts the fabric edges for an ultra-clean finish. However, you need to have the option to engage or disengage the knife, particularly for securing your seams by sewing over previous stitches. This engaging and disengaging must be fairly easy to effect.

You should also pay attention to the weight and dimensions of your serger. Bear in mind that the heavier the machine, the less it will vibrate during serging.

Check how loud it is as well. A serger is certainly not silent, even less so for entry-level models. Some models are noisier than others. If this is an important consideration for you, conduct an internet search.

QUESTION #5:
Is the manual clear?

Before purchasing your serger, make sure that you will have a clear manual available to you. Even better, an in-store demonstration. Look on the web if there are tutorials or videos featuring that particular model. Good, clear, understandable instructions will be indispensable to truly comprehending your machine and having it function perfectly. Manuals are often available online as free PDF downloads. Check out the manual for the model you're interested in to make sure the diagrams and instructions are clear enough.

QUESTION #6:
Does the brand count?

Beyond the brand, you really need to take customer reviews into account. What really works in a brand's favor is its customer service.

QUESTION #7:
What happens if my serger breaks down?

Type "customer service reviews" and the brand name into your search engine. You'll get a lot of results. You can also simply call customer service and see for yourself how long their wait times are. This will give you a first glimpse into the quality of their customer service. Ask yourself as well if it's essential to you to be able to bring your machine in and have a physical person to turn to. If that's the case, it would be a better idea to buy your serger in a shop and not on the internet. Make a note of warranty lengths as well. This is a crucial detail in case of mishaps.

QUESTION #8:
Am I going to have a hard time finding compatible accessories?

With some models, you won't be able to easily find compatible accessories. Check that you'll be able to add, for example, a scrap catcher or easily change the presser foot. To answer this question, visit a fabric store's website and check which brands are available among their selection of serger accessories. Note which brands show up a lot and forget the ones that don't. Be aware that scrap catchers are included with certain models. This is a real plus since sergers produce a lot of scraps. If you don't have a scrap catcher, you're going to spend a lot of time collecting bits of fabric and lint.

QUESTION #9:
What is my budget?

The price of a serger varies a lot, from around $175 to well over $1000. How do you know which price is right? As for many things, the higher the price, the greater the ease of use. Most serging aficionados will advise against purchasing any serger that costs less than $500. But you should know that certain less expensive models can be satisfactory. However, cheaper machines require more time for adjustments.

Don't forget that a serger is an investment, and if everything goes well, it will be with you for decades. It's worth the cost. However, if you don't have the budget, look for used or refurbished models. Check if they are still under warranty. Make sure you have the receipt and complete manual and run a test before buying.

QUESTION #10:
Are there recommended models?

There are many respected brands and models evolve quickly. There is a lot of information and reviews available online and at your local sewing centers. I recommend making a spreadsheet to compare models as you research reviews on the internet.

10 THINGS YOU SHOULDN'T DO with a serger IF YOU DON'T WANT TO DAMAGE IT

MISTAKE #1: using the wrong needles

Read your manual carefully to know which needles you should buy. If the manual says you need to use special serger needles, that means that you can't use regular sewing machine needles. On the other hand, if the manual says you can in fact use universal needles, you have the choice between sewing machine needles and serger needles.

Remember to always use the appropriate needle for your fabric.

MISTAKE #2: using damaged or improperly positioned needles

To know if your needle is damaged or not, you need to check if it's nice and flat. To do this, lay your needle on a flat surface and look to see if it's parallel. Do this test whenever you have any doubt or as a precaution before changing your needle.

Make sure that your needles are always properly positioned. Generally, if the needles are properly installed, the left needle will be slightly higher than the right one. This isn't necessarily enough to guarantee that the needles are placed correctly. It's not always visible to the naked eye. To check, unscrew the needle a little and reposition it.

MISTAKE #3: turning the handwheel in the wrong direction

It can be easy to forget which way to turn the handwheel. As a reminder, its function is to lower or raise the machine's needles. It must always be turned toward you.

MISTAKE #4: forgetting to adjust presser foot pressure

You don't have to adjust this setting every time you sew. However, it's important to pay attention to this adjustment when sewing bulky or lightweight fabrics. For bulky fabrics, we increase the presser foot pressure, and for lightweight fabrics, we decrease it. Pay attention to this setting when you sew these kinds of fabrics and check the manual for advice for your specific machine.

MISTAKE #5: forgetting about differential feed

You need to increase differential feed when sewing very stretchy fabrics in order to avoid gathering them as you sew. You need to decrease this setting when sewing very lightweight fabrics to avoid gathering.

Caution: You should absolutely not touch the differential feed when sewing non-elastic bulky fabrics like denim. Otherwise, you risk damaging your fabric.

MISTAKE #6: messing with the knife

After some time, the fabric may be cut less and less cleanly. You'll notice this right away, as little bits of thread will stick out all along the fabric's edge. Generally, when this happens, it's time to change the knife. I highly recommend you do not attempt this change on your own. The best course of action is to call a dealer. It is actually very easy to damage your machine while changing the knife.

MISTAKE #7: leaving pins in the fabric while sewing

When you do this, you run the risk of your pin coming up against the serger's knife or needles, thus damaging the machine. So remember to remove the pins as you go. Don't forget that the serger moves very fast.

MISTAKE #8: not oiling the machine

It's very important to oil your serger so that it works relatively quietly and doesn't jam. You should do this once or twice a month if your machine sees moderate use. For intensive use, you should oil your serger once a week. Of course, before attempting this maintenance, check in your model's manual for whether or not oiling is advised as well as the recommended frequency.

MISTAKE #9: not covering the machine when not in use

This is a very common mistake. Machines usually come with covers. They protect the machine from dust that can find its way into the tension discs. If this dust accumulates, it can damage your serger.

MISTAKE #10: pulling on the fabric while sewing

It's important to gently draw the fabric with your hand to guide it, but not to forcefully pull or push it.

BUT ALSO

✗ Never block your serger's air vents. Don't place it right up against a wall or pile fabric up behind your machine. Vents should always be clear so your machine doesn't overheat.

✗ Don't place your machine in direct sunlight.

✗ If you need to unplug your machine, don't pull on the power cord while the serger is still turned on. It's better to start by turning off the machine, then removing the power cord.

5 TIPS for keeping YOUR SERGER IN TOP CONDITION

TIP #1: use appropriate materials

Using materials that are not suited to your serger is the number one contributor to its deterioration. Remember to always use the right needles for each type of fabric. Namely, remember to change your needles when sewing stretch fabrics or bulky fabrics. Keep in mind that a damaged needle may cause serious issues with your serger. Remember to change your needles regularly. To make your life easier, you can jot down the date of each needle change and set a reminder for when to replace it. Pay attention as well to the position of the needles. The left should always be higher than the right. They should also be perfectly straight and parallel.

Serger threads last a long time. It's a long-term investment, so don't skimp on quality. A couple extra dollars will avoid the risk of not only damaging your machine but also your stitches. You should also check that the presser foot is correctly placed and that it has no surface irregularities. If it does have irregularities, you will need to change it out so as not to damage your machine or projects.

Make sure to choose accessories that are compatible with your serger. Invest in presser feet from the same brand as your machine. If you have any doubt, ask the retailer to confirm their compatibility. Remember to tighten all the screws on your machine, especially those that secure the needles, as the vibrations produced by your serger can loosen those screws without your knowing it.

TIP #2: pay attention to your fabric

Take note of your fabric's weight and material. You always need to correctly adjust your tensions, stitch width and length, presser foot pressure, and differential feed to suit your fabric. Don't sew fabrics that are too thin or too thick if your machine is not designed for them. It's important to respect your machine's settings and not jump right into sewing without taking the time to make all the necessary appropriate adjustments. Yes, adjusting your serger can take some time depending on your model, but this is essential if you don't want to damage your machine or your work.

TIP #3: regular cleaning

Sergers create a lot of scraps. I recommend cleaning your machine after every project. To clean your machine, turn it off, open the cover, and clean the interior with a large brush. The small brush that comes with the serger is, in my opinion, impractical. I also don't use a vacuum on the mechanisms for fear of sucking up an essential component by mistake. I prefer a large make-up brush to clear out the scraps and lint. However, make sure it doesn't lose any bristles or they may get caught in the machine. Once you have dusted the mechanisms, little scraps will have fallen to the bottom of the machine, so now you can give it a quick vacuum just to collect those fallen pieces. Finally, you can give it a little blast from a can of compressed air to loosen up anything the brush missed.

Think about unplugging your machine whenever you're not using it. And above all, be aware of dust and lint which can create serious though unseen damage. Therefore, in addition to regular cleaning, always remember to use your protective cover.

TIP #4: oil the mechanisms

Sergers have a mechanism that operates at full capacity during every use. Therefore, it's important to regularly oil your machine so that it won't rust over time. A little bottle of oil typically comes with the machine. If not, buy some sewing machine oil. As you only need a drop for each application, this oil should be kept in a cool, dark place so that it lasts a long time.

Before oiling your serger, I recommend checking in your manual whether or not oiling is recommended, as well as which exact components need to be lubricated. As for the frequency of this maintenance, don't wait for your machine to start grinding, but don't go overboard in the other direction either.

TIP #5: pay attention to the knives

Regularly check the condition of the knives. If you notice that little bits of thread remain after serging, then it's time to replace the knives. As a precaution, don't attempt this on your own, but contact a certified repair shop, or else you may damage your machine.

TIP #6: service your machine

We tend to wait for something to go wrong before taking our machines in for service, but an ounce of prevention is worth a pound of cure. Regular service is a check-up performed by a professional. They will be able to verify that the machine is in good working order and will make any necessary adjustments as well as give it a complete cleaning. Inquire at your dealer's, as this maintenance may be covered by your warranty. In general, regular service should be done at least every two years. If your machine sees intensive, semi-professional use, I would advise having it done every year. If your serger sees only occasional use, you don't need to take it in for service. However, I do recommend running your serger at least once a year so it doesn't jam up over time.

EXTRA

Don't forget that servicing your machine can be a good guarantee for reselling your serger. Remember to ask for and save a service record.

QUIZ ANSWERS

QUIZ

Day 1

✘ No, it is not recommended to use the 4-thread overlock stitch on woven fabrics. Instead we use the 3-thread overlock.

✘ The rolled hem.

✘ Yes, you can.

Day 3

✘ This form is specifically suited to the serger's speed, as the thread slides off the top of the cone.

✘ The most frequently used size is no. 120 or 125, which works for any type of serging.

✘ Wooly thread.

Day 4

✘ Yes, you can use them.

✘ False. The higher the number, the better the needle is for thick fabrics.

✘ We use size 80/12 to 90/14 needles.

SHOPPING LIST
SEWING SPECIFIC

Date _____

- ☐ ....
- ☐ ....
- ☐ ....
- ☐ ....
- ☐ ....
- ☐ ....
- ☐ ....
- ☐ ....
- ☐ ....
- ☐ ....
- ☐ ....
- ☐ ....
- ☐ ....
- ☐ ....
- ☐ ....

Modesty Couture

MODESTY COUTURE • ALL RIGHTS RESERVED

Sewing courses to become an expert sewist...

From their studio to yours, Creative Spark instructors are teaching you how to create and become a master of your craft. So not only do you get a look inside their creative space, you also get to be a part of engaging courses that would typically be a one or multi-day workshop from the comfort of your home.

Creative Spark is not your one-size-fits-all online learning experience. We welcome you to be who you are, share, create, and belong.

Scan for a gift from us!

creativespark.ctpub.com